Necessary Chances

Synchronicity in the encounters that transform us

Necessary Chances

Synchronicity in the encounters that transform us

Jeff Vézina

English translation by Carl Anger

Pari
Publishing

www.jfvezina.net/jfv
jf@jfvezina.net

975 Salaberry
G1R 2V4
Quebec, Canada

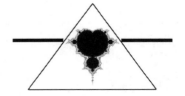

Jeff Vézina describes himself as an explorer of the unconscious. He scans the manifestations of the collective unconscious as seen through cinema, fashions, technological tools, the Internet, his many travels and his private practice. His research themes are relational synchronicity, cinema and psychology, emotional intelligence and the influence of new technologies on human beings.

From 1992 to 1999 he was the president of the Jungian society of Quebec.

In 1996 he obtained his masters degree in clinical psychology from Laval University of Québec, and wrote an essay on the links between chaos theory and Jung.

In 1997, he participated in Peter Wintonick's documentary *The QuébeCanada Complex* for Necessary Illusions Productions, which takes a humorous and psychoanalytic look at the question of Quebec identity.

In 1998 and 1999, he was the producer and host of the radio show *Projections* for CKRL-FM in Quebec City, which examined the relationship between psychology and the cinema.

In 2001 he published the French version (*Les Hasards Nécessaires*) of the book you are about to read. This book quickly became an important reference and sold over 50,000 copies in French and has been translated into Italian and Spanish.

In 2004 he published *Se réaliser dans un mondes d'images: à la recherché de son originalité* in which he develops a unique approach in which we can increase self-knowledge through the films that have marked our lives.

In 2005, he created a psychology and film column for the scientific journal *Cerveau and psyche*, a neuroscience journal published throughout the French-speaking world.

In 2008, he published an innovative and imaginative book about love in which he created a map showing the different regions of a relationship. The book *L'Aventure amoureuse: de l'Amour Naissant à l'Amour Durable* asks the question: What if love is not something but somewhere? He proposes a unique way to find our way when we fall "in love".

Jeff Vézina is also a musician and a composer of electronic music. He composed the digital CD *Projections* and in 2002 completed the soundtrack for the exhibit of the city of Xi'an at Quebec's Museum of Civilization.

"The modern mind is always trying to set limits on life—explaining, demanding rationality, and always looking for what is right and proper. Most conversations about synchronicity focus on physical laws and their aberrations. This book teaches the reader how to live synchronistically. Jeff Vézina opens up fresh ways of making choices—and making sense. I found the book illuminating and liberating."

Thomas Moore, author of *Care of the Soul* and *Writing in the Sand*

"Jeff Vézina has given us a book that develops Jung's theory of synchronicity in a new direction. Owing as much to classical ideas of fulfilling one's destiny as it does to the possibilities of postmodern pluralities, this book offers a perspective on individuation for all of us. By mapping synchronicities in terms of their significance for individuals, Vézina moves the concept away from a mere re-reading of coincidence towards a more spiritual and psychological world view that offers new possibilities all round."

Christopher Hauke is a Jungian analyst in London, and also a writer, film-maker, and Senior Lecturer in applied psychoanalytic studies at Goldsmiths, University of London. He is the author of *Human Being Human: Culture and the Soul* (2005). *Jung and the Postmodern: The Interpretation of Realities* (2000) and editor of *Jung and Film: Post-Jungian Takes on the Moving Image* (2001) and *Contemporary Jungian Analysis: Post-Jungian Perspectives from the Society of Analytical Psychology* (1998). He is editing a new Jung and Film, *The Return,* and writing a new critical introduction to Jung's psychology.

"Relationships are mysterious. Jeff Vézina has opened up a part of this mystery and made it clear. His charming writing style and deep knowledge in *Necessary Chances* will have you experiencing, and viewing, your relationships in a new way."

Bill O'Hanlon, author of *Love is a Verb* and *Rewriting Love Stories*

"Carl Jung gave us the psychology of synchronicity, and Wolfgang Pauli its physics. Now Jeff Vézina has written a delightful anthropology of synchronicity, mapping its interpersonal connections, family ties, and cross-generational streams. A fascinating read!"

Allan Combs, co-author, *Synchronicity: In the Eyes of Science, Myth, and the Trickster*

A catalogue record for this book is available from the British Library
ISBN 978-88-95604-05-3

Book design and cover by Andrea Barbieri

Cover image Copyright © ZDM - Fotolia #7648514

Translation of *Les hasards nécessaires*
First published in French by Éditions de l'Homme
© Editions de l'Homme, 2008
Editions de l'Homme is a division of Groupe Sogides inc.

Printed and bound in Canada

Pari Publishing

Via Tozzi 7, 58045 Pari (GR), Italy
www.paripublishing.com

To Constance Chlore

Table of Contents

Preface

It is a pleasure for me to write the preface to Jeff (J-F) Vézina's *Necessary Chances: Synchronicity in the encounters that transform us*. In particular because Jeff has made a number of visits to our Center here in the medieval Italian village of Pari, times when we have been able to take the opportunity to deepen our discussion on the nature of synchronicity. I knew, of course, of the French edition of his book, first published in 2001, but, thanks to Pari Publishing, Vézina's approach is now available to an English-speaking audience.

While there are other books and essays on Carl Jung's 'meaningful coincidence' Vézina's approach is original in that it lays emphasis on the notion of a meeting or encounter. While in most cases it is an encounter with another individual, it could also involve an encounter with a work of literature, a piece of music, a film, play or work of art. What is most significant about this encounter is its numinous nature and the way it can work to transform the trajectory of an individual's life. By examining a series of such encounters, Vézina deepens our sense of the underlying meaning of synchronicity. He shows that they occur when 'the time is right,' as with the ancient Greek notion of *kairos*. Synchronicities, Vézina argues, can also open us to the future by severing the chains that bind us to the causality of the past.

Indeed the historical development of the very concept of synchronicity is itself the story of a remarkable encounter between two giants in different fields. Wolfgang Pauli was one of the truly outstanding theoretical physicists of the twentieth century, developing his famous Pauli Exclusion Principle, which demonstrated why the different chemical elements can be grouped into families, as well as predicting the existence of the massless, chargeless neutrino twenty-five years before it was experimentally observed.

Pauli was one of the brightest stars in a firmament that included Heisenberg, Dirac, Schrödinger, Bohr and Einstein but around the age of thirty, after his mother's suicide, his life began to fall apart—he drank heavily and began to quarrel with people to the point of being ejected from a bar. In desperation he consulted Carl Jung, who happened to be giving a series of lectures at Pauli's university, the Eidgenössische Technische Hochschule (ETH) in Zurich. It was an encounter that changed Pauli's life in a radical way.

Jung first referred him to Erna Rosenbaum for analysis but later began to work with Pauli on his striking series of dreams, which included a remarkable vision of the World Clock, a symbol of 'the most sublime harmony'. The dreams were also bringing Pauli in touch with his anima who appeared to him as an 'exotic woman'.

While Pauli continued his search for a theoretical approach to unify physics he was also drawn to Jung's universe and began to develop what he termed 'a neutral language,' one that would serve equally for physics and depth psychology, matter and psyche. Clearly his encounter with Jung was having a profound effect, for Pauli began to argue that physics must learn to come to terms with the 'irrational in matter' and that just as Jung had discovered the 'objective side to psyche' with the collective unconscious, so science should discover the subjective side within physics. Likewise he argued that physicists should work 'like the alchemists of old' for their own salvation, and seek the wholeness in nature in order to discover the wholeness within.

But if the encounter changed Pauli what effect did it have on Jung? Pauli believed that Jung's concept of synchronicity was particularly important and encouraged the psychologist to develop and deepen the idea in order to bring greater clarity to the similarities and differences between synchronicity and causality. Indeed it was Pauli who introduced a new definition of 'inconstant connection' to distinguish a synchronistic event from a causal event, one that is always reproducible. Working together, when Jung was in his seventies, Pauli encouraged him to publish his findings which appeared alongside Pauli's own essay on the role of the archetype of the Trinity in the work of Kepler.

Indeed, Pauli felt his own work was so closely linked to Jung's that when a publisher suggested publishing Pauli's essay on Kepler in English, the physicist insisted that it should appear together with Jung's essay on synchronicity. The two essays appeared in 1952 as 'The Interpretation and Nature of the Psyche'.

And so the encounter of the young physicist with the depth psychologist who was approaching his sixties resulted in a significant transformation for both men and also give birth to a concept of synchronicity that had been refined by their many discussions and correspondence. Truly it was a key example of, as the subtitle of Vézina' book has it, one of 'the encounters that transform us'.

F. David Peat   *Pari, Italy, 2009*

Introduction

The world of dream and that of reality certainly share more than appearances would suggest. In the first year of the last century, Freud, in *The Interpretation of Dreams*, showed us how symbolic messages from the unconscious unravel themselves during sleep. But does the unconscious operate only at night and through dreams? Can we also assume that our symbolic life may also extend into waking reality in the form of significant coincidences?

This possibility of symbolic extensions into external reality is at the heart of what the Swiss psychiatrist Carl Gustav Jung introduced with his concept of synchronicity. This concept, worked out jointly with the 1945 Nobel laureate in physics, Wolfgang Pauli, suggests that mind and matter are two aspects of the same tree and that symbols can bloom on the branches of our dreams as much as on those of waking reality.

By pushing the exploration of these links between mind and matter even further, can we suppose that these symbols may at times be manifest through a relationship with another person? The astrophysicist Hubert Reeves, in his book *La synchronicité, l'âme et la science*, asks the question: 'Does an encounter with someone who changes your life have a symbolic meaning?' Can we apply the concept of synchronicity to the small details that lead us to such a person? What would life be like if we hadn't met that particular professor, that author, that man or that woman? What would psychology be like if Jung had not met Freud? What would philosophy be like if Sartre had not met Simone de Beauvoir? History is filled with these highly significant encounters that change a person's life and sometimes the life of a community as well.

We may take a book with us when we go on a trip, but in other cases it is a book that will give us the experience of a major voyage. Likewise, some people may be our companions on our journey through life while others may impact on our life so as to take us on a voyage. Such people are encouraging us to travel to the deepest part of ourselves. They open doors for us. However, as a rule, the most important doors of our existence are opened by those people who will themselves not cross the threshold with us. We probably can all think of someone who suddenly appeared in our life and left an indelible mark. Our relationship with this person may have lasted only a short time. However, we could say that the flutter of his or her wings have set off storms that will determine the course of our existence. Following this encounter, we will never be the same person again.

In this book, I will explore synchronistic encounters; encounters that allow persons, books or other works to enter our lives at determining moments, thus acquiring a symbolic value of transformation. I will also examine symbolic micro-processes. These take the form of thematic patterns or paths that attract and lead us imperceptibly towards a certain person, job, author or country. These patterns unveil themselves in subtle ways. They require the flickering light of our intuition to recognize them and allow us to admire the beauty and uniqueness of life.

The story of how symbolic patterns can unfold within everyday events is one of Jung's major contributions. Given its spectacular and unusual nature, this contribution was unfortunately rejected by scientists or awkwardly simplified by New Age followers. According to the Swiss psychiatrist, it is hard for us to perceive these symbols because our rationality is too bright, just as it is hard for us to perceive stars during the day because the sun is too bright. However, we have a better chance of noticing these stars when we are going through transition periods or when we are entering a chaotic phase in our life. Then the darkness allows these symbolic stars to shine in the form of mysterious synchronicities.

Synchronicity occurs more frequently during periods of psychological tension when the normal symbolic form of the dream has not managed to make itself heard. The psyche must be very 'disturbed' to draw upon an exterior symbol and communicate with us using this medium. Moreover, the message must be particularly important for our development. Synchronicity seen from this angle is not necessarily a 'magic gift,' as it is sometimes described in everyday language, even though suffering can be perceived as a grace. I am always amused when I read the following phrase in a book or article: 'Trigger synchronicity in your lives!' In fact, synchronicity eludes the control of the ego. All you can do is make yourself available to the messages of the unconscious that use this avenue. In a determining phase of our existence, something tries to express itself through synchronicity and we take over from that point in order to hear and decode it.

I will try, using various examples, to illustrate how we can deepen the meaning of a synchronistic event in the same way that we can do so with a dream. I will try to describe how to prepare the ground, especially by developing intuition. However, I would be hard pressed to say how these symbolic flowers can be made to grow faster, as I am not an expert in psychological fertilizers!

Because synchronicity is an abstract notion that points to several dimensions of our existence, I will explore the concept in a specific realm, the interpersonal realm. Since our relationships to others in these times do seem to be particularly 'chaotic,' they may be more easily influenced by disturbances that will bring out symbols in the form of synchronicities. Indeed, issues around relationships are the primary reason for consulting a psychotherapist and the principle factor in bringing about a change.

Since synchronicity is a complex notion, I will use metaphors taken from the science of complexity and chaos theory to produce hypotheses that may help us in the understanding of these concepts. The definition of synchronicity given in the first chapter assumes a very narrow concept of creative chaos found in the recent discoveries of chaos theory. For purists, the term chaos has only a mathematical meaning. However, the etymological origin of the word is linked to the Greek verb to 'gape' or 'yawn'. It is a gulf or abyss. As I conceive it, in terms of interpersonal synchronicity, chaos is this opening, this spontaneous stretching towards another person. It provides oxygen to the soul when boredom begins to set into our lives.

The novel of our life

The determining encounters that mark our personal story or 'novel of our life' do not only happen with people in the flesh. They may also occur in ideas, i.e. the symbols that are part of culture. We have all discovered books, music or movies that changed our existence. These encounters happen at key moments and can resonate with our own personal issues. Synchronistic patterns emerging out of our culture will be examined in terms of the meanings and circumstances that surround the introduction of works that disturb us and at times find a mysterious echo in our own lives.

The place

An encounter inevitably happens within a place. At one level we encounter people throughout our life, but the most significant encounters are with ourselves. This is why special attention will be paid to the places that mark our existence. Places very often symbolize the process of encounter. They take the form of the settings designated by the unconscious in order to indicate coming transformations. We can often read who we are and what we may become in the place where we encounter someone of significance, as well as in the place where we live.

Meaning is the main component of synchronicity. It is an impulse, a direction to give to our own voyage. The metaphors of voyage contained in the present book display the main idea of each chapter and remind us that synchronicity and meaning are intimately linked to the journeys and guidelines that mark our existence. A voyage marks the major changes of our lives as well as it marks each chapter of the present book.

Synchronicity through the generations

The main patterns and themes of our personal novel will very often find their origin in the family novel. The chapter covering life themes that extend over several generations and the analysis of the patterns that maintain themselves over time will complete the present work. We also address the mysterious coincidences of the 'Other inside ourselves' which appear across generations as if they exhibited a strange unconscious loyalty.

Le Visiteur

What space do we make for synchronicity when it suddenly occurs in our life? Even though this book explores a new realm of study—relational synchronicity—it is nonetheless an attempt to understand such a mystery.

Sometimes we face encounters that overwhelm us, that disturb us and lead us to revise our conception of the world. This is expressed in the character of Sigmund Freud in the excellent play written by Eric-Emmanuel Schmitt, Le Visiteur. This play features Freud who, at the end of his life, is visited by a mysterious stranger. We don't really know whether the visitor is a former patient escaped from an asylum or God. This impromptu visitor, who defies all categories, apparently comes out of nowhere, questions Freud on the meaning of his work and disturbs him by relating stunning revelations pertaining to his own life. Among other things, the visitor leads Freud to examine the impact of his pessimism about human nature. He suggests that logic is not the only means to approach reality, which can sometimes be both beautiful and irrational.

Freud, at the time of this visit, is himself very ill. The Gestapo have invaded Vienna and kidnapped his daughter Anna; he is therefore in a very deep state of vulnerability. Unable to explain this visit rationally, he then accuses both the visitor, and irrationality of any kind, of always presenting themselves in the same way—in other words in moments of great weakness and instability. After the visitor performs a magic trick, in which Freud's cane is changed into a bouquet of flowers, the psychologist is at first amazed, then exasperated, and tells him: 'Leave immediately! Not only are you a mythomaniac, but you are suffering from sadistic neurosis. You are a sadist! A sadist enjoying a troublesome night! A sadist who is taking advantage of my weakness.' Then the visitor remarks to Freud:

'If it were not for your weakness, how else could I come in?'

Chapter 1
Unus Mundus

To create is to give shape to one's destiny.
Albert Camus

Human lives are composed like a musical score. Guided by a sense of beauty, Man transforms chance events (a Beethoven composition, a death in a train station) into motifs that become part of his life score. He will return to it, repeat it, modify it, and develop it—as would a composer with the theme of his sonata.
Milan Kundera

Synchronicity has intrigued me for many years. When I completed my training in psychology, I wrote an essay on the link between chaos theory and Jung's theories. Soon after, while on a trip to Prague, I started developing hypotheses on this concept. On the train journey to this pearl of Central Europe, I was jotting down a few ideas in my notebook when an American aged about sixty seated opposite me leaned forward. He had just left his native Detroit and was going to Prague to live with the woman he loved. He was sitting there, in front of me, alone with all his belongings and his hopes. I immediately felt a deep affinity for this man; just like him, I had met a woman living in a faraway city, and I would also have to make a choice.

When I got off the train, I went to a café near the astrological clock at the heart of the city. A stranger started talking to me and at one point mentioned an exhibition on fractals being held at the French Institute in Prague. It seemed a strange coincidence—I was just beginning to take an interest in this subject.

Fractals, a geometry that is scale-independent—small patterns appearing in both the details and the greater picture—is at the core of my synchronistic view of the world. According to this view, patterns that emerge throughout our life story and repeat themselves at different levels of our being make up our *life themes*. These are activated in a special way when we experience encounters. Our 'life score,' as the Czech writer Milan Kundera describes it, is based on just a few motifs; these are played and replayed many times, becoming more intricate with the passage of time, like a fractal.

Our life themes

While on this trip, I walked over the Charles Bridge to go from one bank to the other, pausing in between to contemplate the charming Vltava River. At the time, I was myself at a crossroads, a crucial period of my life, torn between my student life and my career, at the end of one love affair and about to start another.

In times of transition, the unconscious is often more likely to bring about encounters that affect our lives on the symbolic level. These encounters—that we call synchronistic—impose specific themes on us and activate them. It is activated themes that are precisely what we need to integrate into our lives—rather than the person, book or place that has just dazzled us. The latter are nothing more than the symbolic structure, the guise taken by this invitation to transform our inner life.

My discovery of the world of Milan Kundera was one of the changes resulting from my recent encounter with a woman whom I will call Berenice. Thanks to Berenice, I discovered a writer who altered my world view at least as much as this woman had begun to do. Strangely enough, I decided to visit Prague well before becoming familiar with Kundera's books—and I didn't know he was Czech. Berenice, Kundera and Prague: at the time, they made up a theme that was finding its way into my new conception of the world; at the hub of this conception were synchronicity and symbolic manifestations in relationships.

Virtual vertigo

I had met Berenice in a completely unpredictable way, by surfing on the Web. That particular day, I was explaining my research on chaos theory in a discussion group. Berenice happened to be on the same Web site and was intrigued by my discussion. She was convinced I was fooling everyone with my research and sent me a message. That was how we started exchanging emails.

This virtual relationship lasted nine months. Nine months of exchanging words and letters projected on a screen and stored on a hard drive. With this, I could access the very first words, the date, and the time of our initial contact. If we could retrieve our first conversation in a significant relationship, recall the key elements, and decipher them by rebuilding the initial setting and context, we would undoubtedly find in these tiny motifs the major themes of a relational concerto in the making.

In hindsight, after looking over this first discussion with Berenice, I was able to clearly identify the emerging themes. This relationship, initiated through a web of virtual projections, was based mostly on mistrust. Mutual mistrust made up the initial imprint of our relationship. The impression that I was 'toying with her' was already apparent in the first words she used to sound me out; and later on, this impression played itself out on several levels in the relationship. As for me, I was initially fascinated by this 'virtual' woman, but my mistrust transpired into a fear of meeting her 'in person'. I had especially heard (from people in the discussion group on the Web) about her tendency to 'browse' from heart to heart, and this would also become one of the themes of our relationship. 'Browser' and 'mistrust' were part and parcel of this relationship that was establishing itself through the Web.

Having overcome the initial mistrust, i.e. after nine months of virtual pregnancy, we met in the real world. The relationship developed into a passionate affair for nine further months but was terminated abruptly, as is the case with most passionate relationships. No further contact was possible after this break-up.

Synchronistic encounters and symbolic messages

We all meet people who suddenly come into our lives and disappear just as quickly, leaving an indelible mark. They are part of what I call synchronistic encounters and constitute significant passages, as we will see in detail in the next chapter.

The synchronistic aspect of relationships expresses the fact that certain encounters can have a symbolic value in real life, just as with characters in a story or a dream. It also underscores the fact that our relationships convey symbolic messages.

Despite these symbolic markers, however, our life's work is a sketch that will never be finished. We are constantly faced with decisions we must make, yet we cannot determine at the time if we have made the 'right choice'. Indeed, we cannot know where the paths we have not taken would have led us. It can be mind-boggling to consider all the choices (conscious or unconscious) we have to face on a daily basis. Did the American from Detroit that I met on the train—abandoning it all for a woman—make the right decision? And Tomas, in Kundera's *The Unbearable Lightness of Being*, who returns to Prague to be near Tereza and becomes a window washer—does he make the right decision? What about myself, deciding to stay in Quebec City rather than follow Berenice—did I make the right choice?

The bee—an example of a synchronistic symbol

Though we are never certain of having made the 'right choice,' the unconscious sometimes uses symbols, in periods of uncertainty and questioning, to 'show' us a meaning. This can be conveyed through a synchronistic experience, especially during key transitions or phases of our lives. For example, one of the symbolic motifs of my relational concerto with Berenice took the form of a bee. Strangely enough, when we met, bees were already present as small, barely 'audible,' symbolic motifs. Often, during our walks together, bees would buzz around us.

As Berenice had refused to come and live with me, I had to make a choice: pursue my career as a psychologist in Quebec City (a career that was just starting out but was a promising one thanks to the network I had developed), or abandon everything just like the American I met in Prague and go live with Berenice.

It was probably the hardest decision I had to take in all my life. My gut feeling was that her heart was about to flee towards another man. I ended up staying in Quebec City, and that was the end of our relationship. On the day following my decision, a bee came into my room through the window, flew over my bed and woke me up. I paid little attention to this small, amusing incident. But then, a few weeks later, I noticed a dead bee lying near my bed. To my astonishment, the insect had a red hair wrapped around its body. I knew the hair belonged to Berenice, as she had changed her hair color to red just before our break-up. When I saw the poor little insect entangled in the red hair, I was in a state of intense fascination—a state typical of a synchronistic experience. This state can be compared to the finale of a moving concerto: a deep feeling of oneness momentarily reconciles us with ourselves and with life in general. A few days after finding the bee and the red hair, I discovered all my belongings that were still in Berenice's possession on my doorstep; she had dropped them off while in Quebec City. The unconscious had chosen this image (the dead bee entwined in the red hair) to symbolize the themes of our relationship and help me accept this break-up.

We had for a time managed to attain a greater level of intimacy, momentarily sweeping away the initial mistrust. I associate this coming closer together with hair. Hair is a symbol of intimacy in most cultures. Brushing someone's hair, for example, is a gauge of trust and togetherness. Despite our attempts at coming closer together and developing intimacy between us we, had not managed to get rid of our initial wariness. A red hair wrapped around a dead bee conveyed our inability to enter into a relationship.

Bees are also evocative of Berenice's flighty attitude, an attitude that increased my doubts and made me want to keep my distance. Bees are particularly symbolic of resurrection and associated with the rites of initiation: 'At Eleusis and Ephesus, the priestesses are called bees. They are represented on tombs as signs of the afterlife.'[1] The bee, an insect that indeed changes pollen into honey, illustrated for me the 'initiatory' and symbolic nature of this relationship—and this transformed my vision of the world.

Some critical readers may think the meaning I ascribe to synchronicity stemmed from the need to relieve my distress, after deciding to end the relationship. The meaning given to a synchronistic event is of course partly subjective, and coincides with a period of questioning and 'weakness'—to use the metaphor from the play Le Visiteur, summarized in the Introduction. But this is true of any statistical result or objective piece of data that we interpret.

Yet the meaning that emerges from synchronicity cannot be exclusively subjective, as it has an observable effect. It generates a highly emotional energy and leads to transformations in periods of transition and questioning. The meaning of synchronicity takes root deep in the collective unconscious, at a level that Jung calls the objective psyche,[2] and becomes conscious as a phenomenon—as natural as a flower growing in a field. The psyche produces symbols as naturally as nature produces flowers. We can take several different postures regarding this natural phenomenon: we can pick the flower, smell its fragrance, write a poem about it, or even analyze its chemical properties, take it apart and attempt to clone it. When it comes to synchronicity, it all depends on the observer and his/her relationship to the world. It creates a relationship to a unified and symbolic world as in a fairy tale or dream.

---

1   Jean Chevalier, *Dictionnaire des symboles*, Robert Laffont, Paris, 1982, p. 1.

2   The objective psyche is the deepest part of the collective unconscious where contents are all inter-related into an undifferentiated unity.

From synchronicity to black holes

Jung developed the concept of synchronicity with his friend the Nobel Laureate Wolfgang Pauli. Pauli was especially keen on experimenting with all types of synchronicities. Jung once declared that he had rarely met someone whose unconscious was as disturbed as Pauli's. In addition, several of Pauli's dreams were transcribed in Jung's book *Psychology and Alchemy*. This was an attempt to describe the archetypal scope of Pauli's dreams by establishing a parallel with alchemy, a very important process of transformation in the Middle Ages. Recently, the publication of the correspondence between the two men (which extended over a quarter of a century) has shed light on one of the most brilliant exchanges of letters of the twentieth century. In this intense correspondence, we are party to the development of Jung's most complex concept.

The concept of synchronicity was developed with particular thoroughness over a period of several years yet remained incomplete. Jung conceived the idea of synchronicity fairly early in his career, in particular during a series of dinners with Albert Einstein around 1920. As suggested by this quote from Jung, taken from the Foreword of his correspondence with Pauli, Einstein apparently inspired him in the following way: '… Professor Einstein was my guest on several occasions at dinner… It was Einstein who started me off thinking about a possible relativity of time as well as space and their psychic conditionality. More than thirty years later, this stimulus led to my relationship with the physicist Professor W. Pauli and to my thesis of psychic synchronicity.'

Jung developed the notion of synchronicity by starting from the idea of a collective unconscious, which can be summarily defined as a *field of fundamental possibilities* inherited from the long shared history of experiences of the human species. This field exerts its influence in the same way as gravity, but its range of influence is situated outside the limits of time and space. It purportedly attracts our perceptions and emotions through its 'attractors'—the archetypes—, and incites us to take action in a particular direction.

For example, when we see a woman, we unconsciously associate this *woman* with *Woman*, i.e. the Anima archetype. From the beginning, humanity has experienced womanhood, and this relationship has created symbolic motifs in the collective unconscious that can be observed indirectly through various cultural representations—everything from Virgin to Witch. Thus, humanity, through its archetypes, possesses symbolic themes that repeat and fashion themselves over the course of history. Each one of us also possesses personal themes that repeat themselves and can take the form of *complexes*. A cluster of complexes is a way of bringing together related events, ideas and emotions, just as we group the stars when we gaze at the night sky. Complexes are more specific life themes, bringing our more personal preoccupations into focus. For example, someone with an abandonment complex will probably be obsessed with the idea of losing his/her loved ones. This sensitive zone could become a focus for the creation of symbols. These symbols can lead to synchronicity, providing an overall meaning to the pathways of life.

In this matrix of possibilities represented by the collective unconscious, archetypes are somewhat like nodes—black holes or attractors that relate to the repetition of collective experiences. These nodes are not directly perceived by us, just as we cannot perceive black holes. It is therefore impossible to clearly distinguish an archetype. Neither is it possible to photograph a black hole. We can find a black hole in the cosmos by observing the way light is diverted nearby. A complex or archetype is discovered in the same way, i.e. when *emotional energy is diffracted.*

Jung drew on a notion from the alchemists of the Middle Ages. This is the idea of *unus mundus*, the 'one' world, illustrating how the psychic sphere coincides with the physical sphere. Thus, in the deepest part of the collective unconscious, mind and matter, time and space are not separated. A person who experiences synchronicity seems to come in contact with this dimension of *unus mundus*.

Recent discoveries in quantum mechanics have shed light on the grand unity of nature. The inseparable and non-local properties of matter were demonstrated in brilliant fashion in physics by theories and experiments that arose out of a paradox proposed by Einstein, Podolsky and Rosen (the EPR paradox). In seeking to resolve this paradox, John Bell showed, at the quantum levels, that particles that were correlated continue to remain so even when separated by distances of several kilometers. To demonstrate this paradox in the laboratory, two particles are coupled together, then separated by a great distance. It was discovered that when one particle was stimulated, the other would react instantaneously, as if the two particles had never been separated. Everything seems to be related to everything, as if matter and mind were part of the same tree. Synchronicity would then be an opening in the roots that connect the individual to the whole; this key moment allows us to experience the fact that we are a living paradox—at once 'one' and 'all'.

In this sense, the concerto form in music wonderfully illustrates the phenomenon of synchronicity. The concerto is made up of a solo instrument that interacts with an orchestra. It draws near, melds with, then veers away from the orchestra, like the movement of an individual who tries to embrace the waves and rhythmic pulses of the musical score played by the collective unconscious.

Implicate order

The physicist David Bohm came up with an interesting hypothesis that can be related to synchronicity by means of his idea of *implicate* and *explicate* order. His theory implies the existence of a unified, hidden order that unfolds itself according to certain patterns. These patterns manifest themselves through forms that we perceive in reality. According to Bohm's idea, synchronicity would therefore include patterns that transcend time and space by taking root in the implicate order. In this underlying order, everything is unified and contained in embryonic form, as in the *unus mundus*. We can also find this idea in fractals as well as in holograms, in which one small part contains the whole image. Holograms can be found, for example, on credit cards, images that create an illusion of three dimensional depth. Moreover, when a hologram is broken, each fraction contains within it the entire image.

In Bohm's conception, the movement going from implicate order to explicate reality is called a *holomovement*; it is somewhat like a broken 'hologramic' mirror, in which particles of a whole take the form of individual phenomena that can be perceived by our senses. The self perceives reality in a fragmented way, but these fragments—physical phenomena— are apparently nothing but energy condensations. The particles that currently make up our bodies are the same ones that have existed since the Big Bang. For example, when we die, the carbon in our bodies—a substance that is present throughout nature in plants, animals, stones, etc.—will continue to exist in another form. This is how we inscribe our identity into this flux, this holomovement of nature and being. The self can thus be seen as a sort of wave in the ocean of reality. This hypothesis helps us understand how mental patterns form and coincide with physical patterns; this is what is observed when synchronicity binds the implicate order more tightly with explicate reality.

Collective knowledge

The notion of morphogenetic fields, developed by Rupert Sheldrake, can also help us to understand synchronicity. This theory supposes that collective knowledge is accessible to any individual and can arise in any given group. It was developed in particular using a study of the behavior of monkeys. Scientists gathered a colony of monkeys on an isolated island in the Pacific Ocean and taught them to wash their potatoes before eating them. The monkeys in the colony succeeded in executing this ritual exercise. After several years, the scientists realized that monkeys from neighboring islands—who had never come in contact with the original island monkeys—had also started washing their potatoes before eating them. Sheldrake thus advanced the hypothesis that a morphogenetic field was at play; it facilitated learning and became operational after a few years. Though this hypothesis is an interesting one in itself, the theory is controversial. It is indeed difficult to prove objectively that such fields exist. The hypothesis that 'collective knowledge exists at the unconscious level' is at the core of synchronicity. However, this knowledge may have taken several thousands years to develop. It is therefore difficult to establish that such a field could be set up in just a few short years.

I refer the reader who would like to explore these hypotheses in greater detail to more specialized books on this topic. Books by physicists F. David Peat[3] and Victor Mansfield[4] explore these themes more explicitly. This book will borrow more from the notions of chaos theory and complexity science in order to bring out a few new ideas for understanding synchronicity. First of all, however, here is a definition of synchronicity using a famous example by Jung.

A definition

Although I want to avoid associating synchronicities with insects, I will nonetheless describe the typical (I would even say canonical) example of synchronicity using the example of the scarab beetle. I use this example because it will allow me to give a clear definition of synchronicity.

> *Jung had an extremely rational client who had been in therapy for a long time. She rejected all interpretations and stubbornly resisted treatment. During a session, the client referred to a dream she had had in which she received a golden scarab beetle as a present. At the precise moment when the client was reciting her dream, a scarab-type insect, a rose chafer, bumped into the window loudly enough to grab Jung's*

3   F. David Peat, *Synchronicity: The Bridge Between Matter and Mind*, Bantam Books, New York, 1987.

4   Victor Mansfield, *Synchronicity, Science and Soul Making*, Open Court, Chicago, 1995.

and his client's attention. Jung stood up, took the insect and dropped it in front of the client. The client was stunned and only then started to respond to the therapeutic process.

Starting from this example, the definition I propose for synchronicity is as follows:

Synchronicity is a coincidence between an inner (subjective) and exterior (objective) reality in which events are related through meaning, i.e. in acausal fashion. This coincidence sets off a strong emotional energy in the person experiencing it and indicates a state of deep transformations. Synchronicity occurs in periods of deadlock, questioning and chaotic upheaval.

Four clues or indicators help distinguish a typical synchronicity arising from this definition.

1. There is no acausal connection; the connection between the events is arrived at through meaning.

2. This coincidence sets off a strong emotional charge in the person experiencing it, suggesting a cluster of symbolic images. This energy denotes the *numinous*[5] aspect of the experience, the feeling that the person is being summoned by the unconscious.

3. This coincidence reveals transformations in the person, hence the symbolic value of synchronicity.

4. It normally happens when the person is in a transitional, chaotic or deadlocked situation. This state refers to the *liminal* (from the Latin *limen* meaning threshold) dimension of the experience.

Synchronicity is a vast concept but this definition applies particularly to synchronistic encounters. Indeed, synchronistic experiences strangely resemble that of falling in love, or having a significant encounter that transforms our lives. When we fall in love, the self's boundaries are momentarily wiped out—the external mixes with the internal world, and vice versa. As with synchronicity, a budding love affair is more likely to take place following a period of emptiness in an individual's life, or during transition periods, as Alberoni so aptly described in *Falling in Love*: 'No

---

5 A numinous experience is one that is associated with an 'aura,' as if it were surrounded by 'light'. It is as if such an occurrence is actually 'directing us' so as to create a feeling that we are being 'seen in the experience'.

one can fall in love if he or she is even partially satisfied with what he or she has or who he or she is. The experience of falling in love originates in an overwhelming depression, an inability to find anything good about one's everyday life.'[6] Indeed, much like synchronicity, one feature of nascent love is that it unlocks a seemingly deadlocked situation—and it does this in acausal fashion, i.e. completely spontaneously. We become receptive to love, as well as change and synchronicity.

Synchronicity acumen

To distinguish synchronicity from simple coincidences, we need to identify precise criteria for synchronicity and avoid jumping too quickly to conclusions. To illustrate a coincidence that does not meet the criteria of synchronicity, Michel Cazenave, the French philosopher and writer, in a talk on synchronicity, gave the following example experienced by his son Tristan. I will reproduce his example here. Note that his son was born on May 26, 1968.

> *One day, Cazenave found a letter convening his son to an admissions exam at a university. This summons concerned a certain Tristan Cazenave, born May 26, 1968. He gave the document to his son saying that he didn't know his son had signed up to study at that particular university. His son looked at the document and told his father it wasn't for him; he had never made such an application. Cazenave returned the letter and called the university. He then learned that another Tristan Cazenave was living in France and was born on the same day of the same year. Intrigued, he checked the hour of birth of both: the two births were one minute apart!*

In this case, there is no emotional impact on Tristan Cazenave's life (second criterion) nor any meaning relating the two realities or events (first criterion). There is no transformation brought about by the coincidence, and no one was in a deadlock (third and fourth criteria). Despite the unlikelihood of the event, it is not a synchronicity. Coincidences can occur without necessarily being synchronistic. This type of coincidence is called a worldly coincidence; the concept was developed in particular by Paul Kammerer and will be examined later.

---

6   Francesco Alberoni, *Falling in Love*, Random House, New York, 1983, p. 108.

Acausality, the first point of the definition of synchronicity, indicates that events are related through meaning and not causality. It is therefore wrong to look for causes of coincidences. What we need to look for is this: what dialogue can we engage in with ourselves and with life as a whole with respect to the synchronistic event. Acausality, or the requirement of meaning, is an order of experience as important as causality in nature; but it is only accessible at special moments, i.e. critical periods.

The second part of the definition of synchronicity concerns the emotional factor. It is an intense sensation, similar to when we awaken from a long dream. The emotional impact takes us in one particular direction, and generally drives us to write something, or inspires us to do something constructive. For example, this book was marked by many synchronicities, and the one concerning the bee strongly prompted me to begin writing it.

Symbolically charged archetypes lead individuals down certain paths. In Chapter 5, we will see how a strong emotional charge activates an archetype, putting us in more intimate contact with the knowledge inscribed in the collective unconscious. In the case of the scarab beetle, the archetypal nature of the synchronicity refers back to collective history, and in particular that of the Egyptians. According to the ancient Egyptians, the scarab beetle was principally associated with transformation. Scarab beetles transform and reproduce themselves in an odd fashion. First of all, the adult scarab beetle drops its eggs in sheep excrement. It then pushes the mixture into a ball and rolls it around until it finds a source of water. When it locates a source, it throws the ball into the water. Some time later, a new scarab beetle emerges from this small package of water-logged excrement. Egyptians probably observed this phenomenon and this no doubt explains why they associated the scarab beetle with transformation. There is another image of 'excrement' which undergoes a transformation. This image is associated with the alchemists' tradition. In this case, excrement is symbolically transmuted into gold. It is, in fact, a metaphor reminding human beings that they have the power to improve their lot by undergoing a transmutation, changing what appears negative into something positive.

The third aspect of the definition of synchronicity concerns changes brought about by a synchronistic experience. The goal is to discover how an event can transform us. In the example of Jung's client, the famous scarab beetle helped 'unlock' the therapy session. Synchronicity can therefore be seen as an act of creation in time; it leads to a change, a transformation.

The fourth and final aspect of synchronicity deals with the in-between state; the tension or deadlock we experience when synchronicity occurs. In the example of the scarab beetle, the patient had stopped making progress and was in a deadlock. If we are in a period of uncertainty, if we feel we are at an impasse, we will be predisposed to experience synchronicity. This in-between state conjures the archetype of Mercury (Hermes in Greek mythology), the archetype of passages, the one linking the conscious to the unconscious. It is also the archetype of movement and travel associated with the Trickster, the mischievous demon who meddles with our lives to help us expand our world vision.

It should be noted, however, that this in-between aspect does not actually trigger synchronicity. Rather, it is a state that predisposes the individual to live this type of experience. It is not enough for an individual to be in a state of uncertainty, turmoil or chaos for synchronicity to occur in his or her life.

We need to reiterate at this point that when synchronicity occurs, we are under the influence of an acausal order. This in-between concept is very well illustrated in the following example.

The unicorn

Michelle, a woman in her forties, was confronted with making a choice. Here is the dream she had:

> I see a magician with the power to repair broken horns on unicorns. I see a unicorn without a horn. The magician attaches the horn on its head and it welds itself as if by magic. I am full of admiration for this man, but I find out afterwards that I am in fact watching a film, and that this magician is not real, he is just an actor. I feel an intense deception on realizing that he is just a character in a movie.

Following this, Michelle reported the following:

> When I woke up, I walked by the fireplace on which stood a glass unicorn that I friend had given to me a long time ago. Just as I walked by, the unicorn fell to the floor and broke into several pieces. The horn was also broken. The dream then came back to me vividly.

> At that time, I had just changed my lifestyle. I had for a long time lived on the edge of society and this life depressed me.

I had just moved to a new city (I had the dream one week after my move) where I hoped to find a job and start having a social life. However, I had just met a man who was living an unconventional lifestyle who asked me to follow him to the south of France to live in a commune. I faced the following dilemma: follow this man and remain an outside or start living by myself in my new apartment. The man came to see me after the dream. After much thought, I decided to put an end to our relationship. It was a wise decision. A few weeks later, I met the person who is my life companion today.

When Michelle had this synchronistic experience, she was in an *in-between* state. We can assume that this coincidence between dream and reality helped 'guide' her life choices. When dealing with a problem, the unconscious has a more extended set of data it can access than the conscious self, and it can resolve the problem by the use of symbols. In Michelle's example, the unconscious was able to detect the lying magician in the person of the 'unconventional' man; it generated a double symbol—applying it both to the dream and to reality—to 'protect' the dreamer from eventually having a relationship with him.

The unconscious can condense certain aspects of our relationships into symbols that can be deployed in real life. Extracting the underlying meaning from these symbols is an on-going task. It is not directly accessible, and neither is the archetype that supports it.

Chance, snowflakes and dice games

Jung, the father of the concept of synchronicity, never stated that chance did not exist. With his notion of archetype,[7] however, he did develop the necessary roundabout paths—the inevitable routes taken by the psyche—that are activated and oriented in a certain direction during synchronicity. Despite all the options available to it, the psyche seems to naturally choose certain paths, leading an individual to make specific encounters at precise moments in his or her life. According to this model, our lives unfold somewhat like snowflakes. Snowflakes always have six points[8]—a

---

7   An archetype is a pattern from the collective unconscious that leads us to perceive the world in a certain way and influences our actions.

8   This is of course a metaphor. I don't claim here that there are only six life themes. An undetermined number of these themes, however, condition our lives by repeating themselves.

metaphor for the cluster of themes in life that attract synchronicities. Inside the snowflake, however, random variations abound, just like the details of our lives.

Life, and the encounters that make up our existence, consist of a combination of order and chaos, chance and determinism. If life did not engage in 'play,' it would be much more predictable—in the end, rather boring. In addition, it would lack creativity and be a great deal less beautiful. Chance is therefore a creative trial-and-error principle, a principle of variation that gives life its beauty—the same life that creates snowflakes.

According to Jung and Pauli, however, the dice are sometimes loaded. Their great discovery, with synchronicity, is precisely that meaning is the greatest 'dice loader,' for it can change the course of events that are usually driven by causality and determinism. It seems that certain chance events organize themselves through meaning.

Try observing children playing in a park who don't know each other; they play alone at first, then gradually join together and invent games often with very precise rules and a well-defined purpose. But the possibility always exists that some children will play alone, aimlessly. Similarly, there are chance occurrences and highly improbable phenomena with no specific cause, no meaning or finality for the self experiencing them, nor any power of transformation. These chance events are somewhat like children who decide to play alone.

Then there are chance events that organize themselves through meaning and become necessary chances, synchronicities. Synchronicity is therefore definitely very close to chance.

The sacred risk of chance

Chance is measured by its degree of improbability.[9] Its improbability arises from the fact that we are unaware of its causes or lack of causes, as in the case of an acausal synchronistic event. An unlikely event can provide a lot of information by forcing us to question our existence. As Kundera emphasizes: 'Only chance can be interpreted as a message. That which happens by necessity, that which is expected and repeats itself daily has nothing to say. Only chance speaks to us. We try to read it like gypsies read the patterns left by grounds inside a coffee cup.'[10]

Chance is necessary to life and is an effective strategy for making a new order emerge creatively in nature. When a fortuitous event throws a person, an animal or a cell off-balance, for example through synchronicity or an unforeseeable blow, the element that is perturbed will naturally try to regain its balance. Without the chaos of unforeseeable events, there can be no balance. According to Boris Cyrulnik, the father of the resilience concept (the physical property of a material that regains its shape after a shock), any such shock is bearable as long as the subject is able to express it in the form of a narrative. In the case of human beings, looking for underlying meanings in the chance events of synchronicity is part of the process of regaining one's balance.

Chance is the playful aspect of life that helps someone get back on his/her feet and into motion, when he or she manages to incorporate it into a narrative. 'Chance favors only those who are well prepared,' as Pasteur said.

Kammerer's Law of Seriality and Coincidences

Certain coincidences that seem highly unlikely and have unknown causes can be linked together without any apparent meaning. These are, however, not true synchronicities. Paul Kammerer, an Austrian biologist who lived in the first part of the twentieth century, was fascinated by events in life that repeated themselves. For example, imagine yourself taking a bus with a ticket bearing the number 2745, then going to a restaurant and finding the same number on your bill. Then you meet someone whose telephone number has the same numbers, and so on. This is exactly the kind of coincidence that fascinated Kammerer. He

---

9   Milan Kundera, *Immortality*, HarperCollins, New York, 1999.

10 Milan Kundera, *The Unbearable Lightness of Being*, 1984. [My translation CA]

---

spent entire days seated in public places making observations in order to identify these types of coincidences. His observations led him to develop a law of seriality. His work was published in 1919 under the name *Das Gesetz der Serie* (The Law of Seriality).

Kammerer listed about 100 cases that he grouped meticulously. He distinguished between the number and strength of coincidences. The number denotes the frequency, i.e. the number of times the event is reproduced, and the strength corresponds to the number of parallels that can be drawn between events.

Among his observations, Kammerer gives an example of two 19-year-old soldiers, born in the same city (Silesia), unknown to each other, who are both admitted to the same hospital in 1915, are both stricken by pneumonia, and both have the name Franz Richter.

Most of the examples given by Kammerer are very amusing, but do not go beyond worldly coincidences. Kammerer's book is no longer available, but you can read a summary of his work in Arthur Koestler's book *The Case of Midwife Toad*, a sort of biography of Kammerer. In this book, we learn about Kammerer's dramatic death. He lost an important quantity of data and observations as a result of the First World War. Humiliated by the scientific community, he committed suicide in 1926.

Kammerer's law of series is now forgotten though it was one of the first attempts to 'scientifically' examine the phenomenon of coincidences. This Law of Seriality is useful in helping us understand one aspect of synchronicity: the creation of nodes and recurring patterns in a network of events. However, these nodes do not necessarily have meaning and are not synchronicities.

Thinking big in a small world

The theory of 'six degrees of separation' is another approach of coincidences. I became familiar with this theory in a rather synchronistic way, thanks to the filmmaker Vali Fugulin, who made a documentary *six. lemondeestpetit.ca*, produced by the National Film Board of Canada.

Vali Fugulin started out by contacting a psychoanalyst friend to learn more about synchronicity. That day, I happened to be at this person's place in Montreal to take part in a television show on synchronicity. After answering the filmmaker's questions, he mentioned my name. I talked with Fugulin, and she asked me to appear in her documentary. Several months later, I was informed of the recording date for this interview, which was to take place in Montreal. To my astonishment, the recording was on the very day I was giving a lecture in Montreal. This coincidence was rather stunning; at the time, I only rarely traveled to this city. And on the day of the official screening of the documentary, I was again in Montreal for another television show on synchronicity.

Vali Fugulin, who has since reappeared repeatedly in my life, told me about this theory of six degrees of separation of which I knew nothing— a theory that allowed me to deepen my understanding of synchronicity.

We all know the expression 'It's a small world'. This expression perfectly illustrates the theory of six degrees of separation, developed by Harvard sociologist Stanley Milgram. To demonstrate his theory, Milgram began a research study in 1967 in which he asked participants from Kansas and Nebraska to send letters to Boston residents by relying only on acquaintances likely to know these people. The letter had to be delivered by hand and travel through a human network. He realized that it took on average six go-betweens for a letter to arrive at its destination; this was the case even if the people targeted lived in cities as far apart as Boston and Kansas City.

According to this theory, if I write a letter to a person selected at random and give this letter to friends likely to know the person, it will take on average six intermediate persons to get delivered. In other words, it often takes no more than six people to reach anyone in the world. The NFB documentary filmmaker repeated the experiment and arrived at the same conclusions as Milgram, using individuals from Montreal who connected to addressees as far away as Japan through less than six intermediaries!

This theory also borrows from recent discoveries on the emergence of order in networks, as we will see in Chapter 4. These show that in a vast network of individual elements, we can observe the emergence of catalysts—shortcuts, as it were—within the complexity. This principle of fractal organization is also how blood is distributed throughout the body, how viruses propagate in a population, and even how rumors spread in a small town. Again, the missing element here is the dimension of meaning, with meaning these catalysts could emerge in a unique way into a network of synchronistic events.

Chance and fate

These two theories show us that all coincidences are not necessarily synchronicities. The issue of chance and coincidences is a complex and delicate one. A world view in which chance did not exist would be a sad one. If chance did not exist and all was predetermined through unmitigated fate, individuals would have no room for free will and maneuvering.

The leeway we have for realizing our destiny is related to consciousness. The more an individual is aware of themes that personalize his or her life, the more he or she is free to make creative choices. Conversely, the less an individual is conscious of vulnerable aspects, the more harshly destiny will impose itself. As Jung wrote: 'When an inner situation is not made conscious, it happens outside, as fate'.

To open up this creative free space, synchronicity sometimes provides us with dice that are loaded with meaning. It channels chance events through paths that facilitate our quest for meaning in our lives. Notwithstanding my theoretical attempts here, however, it is a tricky issue to clearly distinguish between chance and synchronicity. Life sometimes operates with a sense of humor, and frowns on categories. The examples that make up this book will provide a framework for exploring the concept in a more useful way than would more elaborate theoretical developments.

We must take care to avoid 'seeing meanings everywhere,' like the character in the film *Signs and Wonder* by Jonathan Nossiter. Synchronicity should not be a way of denying our ability to play with life by developing unhealthy superstitions, like the character in this film.

It would be an oversimplification to say that all chance events have a meaning and are synchronistic. Meaning can only exist if we admit the possibility that the event could also be meaningless. Some absurd chance events can be resolved through creativity, but they have no hidden meaning. Someone going through a trying event can be hurt by statements such as: 'You know, this disaster did not happen to you without a reason'. It is only natural to try to use experiences to our advantage; but if this quest for order and meaning is simply rational, we may be restricting our options and lacking creativity.

'Order is in man's spirit, not in nature,' as the psychiatrist Guy Ausloos so aptly said.[11] To approach synchronicity, we must learn to tolerate uncertainty and let ourselves be moved by the mysteries of the unlikely. To let this natural dimension enter our lives, a strict and rational order must be sacrificed in many cases—an order that is very often overturned by the chaos of encounters that transform us.

---

11 Guy Ausloos, *Compétence des familles: Temps, chaos et processus*, Érès, Paris, 1995.

Chapter 2
Synchronistic Encounters

If the soul wants to recognize itself, it will have to look at the soul of the Other.
    Plato

Love is when differences no longer separate us.
    Jacques de Bourbon Busset

The night of December 31, 1999, was especially significant in my life. I had decided to experience the new millennium in Egypt, at the *Twelve Dreams of the Sun* concert, presented by French musician Jean-Michel Jarre in front of the pyramids. This concert was without a doubt the most intense cultural and symbolic event I have ever witnessed. The rhythms of the dumbeks and darbookas, combined with the lazy, meandering sounds of the rababs, worked well in combination with the delicate pulse of the modern synthesizers. I could not have dreamed that such a clash of diverse cultures and musical styles could create such a vibrant feeling of unity.

A few days before the Jarre concert, I visited an isolated neighborhood of Cairo. I had my concert ticket but as the writing looked like spaghetti to me, I asked someone at the French Cultural Center in Cairo to authenticate it. It was there that I met a very friendly couple from Quebec. They were in love and were to be married in Egypt at the hour of the new millennium. After our conversation, we agreed to attend the concert together, and they gave me the name of their hotel. With this information in hand, I planned to meet up with them before the concert. I never managed to find their hotel, though, and so was unable to meet them at the concert.

As often happens on a trip, I met this couple again by chance while walking in the suburbs of Cairo on December 31. Cairo is a city of several million people, probably the most densely populated city of Africa and the Arab world. This coincidence was therefore very intriguing. The two Quebecois were going to Saqqara to visit the first Step Pyramid built by the architect Imhotep. As I had already visited this monument, we parted and agreed on meeting at the entrance of the pyramids at the end of the afternoon. Setting up a meeting in this way was probably the best way of never seeing each other again. Despite my best efforts, my tiny, individual will was no rival to the chance circumstances that had set them on my path a second time, right in the middle of the suburbs of Cairo. I never saw this couple again. I would have liked to think it was a synchronistic encounter, but their brief passage in my life had not changed my existence. This coincidence simply made me realize that what appears to be a synchronistic encounter can be the result of random, unnecessary events; we must be very careful when examining synchronicity in our relationships to other people.

The encounter

I am often overcome by a feeling of powerlessness when people come to me in therapy, trying to find out 'what to do' to meet the right person. There is no magic method for setting up a major encounter. I maintain that important encounters in our lives cannot be prearranged. A significant encounter between two people remains a mystery—the laws of causality and probability are of no use here. In fact, it may be an illusion to believe that the harder we try, the better our chances are of meeting this special person.

Something similar is happening with the computerization of society. We thought a profusion of information would help us make the right choices. Instead, we are witnessing an unexpected turn of events: the overabundance of information. This information overload is in fact a type of pollution that may inhibit our ability to choose. What is useful, in this case, is information that startles us, driving us out of our vegetative state as we attempt to make it our own. Information does not necessarily lead to knowledge. Knowledge comes from information that we integrate over time, just as getting to know someone takes time. 'It is the time you have spent on your rose that makes your rose so important,' as Saint-Exupéry said.

We are experiencing a similar state of affairs in our relationships to other people. Encounters are fast and plentiful and act like a surplus of information. They can lead to a superficial attitude, often hindering our chances of really meeting someone.

On the same wavelength

Indeed, there have never been so many ways of meeting people as there are today. The standard dating agencies, telephone dating services, and chatlines on the Web are all ways of bringing people together quickly and easily. Moreover, new dating agencies are planned that will use electronic chips programmed like tamagotchis. Tamagotchis are those small electronic pets that are so popular with kids. Kids take care of their essential needs such as eating, sleeping, protecting them, acting just like a parent would. The new generation of tamagotchis requires that the user also takes care of emotional needs and relationships. These new pets have a chip that the child can program according to his or her personality and preferences. It is equipped with a radio transmitter-receiver that broadcasts on a preset frequency. When one of these pets comes within a few meters of another tamagotchi with a compatible radio frequency, the chip acts to sound a bell. The two children can meet through their pets. Based on this concept, we can imagine a new type of cell phone in the near future with a chip for detecting 'compatible partners' nearby!

Notwithstanding all these artificial means of dating, are we really able to meet someone who will be significant to us? Despite all the ways at our disposal for curtailing the chance element in our encounters and bringing it under the rule of reason, are we in a position to make the right choices?

In a talk given in Quebec City, Ignacio Ramonet,[12] the editor of *Le Monde diplomatique,* pointed out that market and technology mechanisms are increasingly infiltrating personal relationships: we choose our life partners in much the same way as we buy our groceries, leaving less and less room for intuition and chance in order to consume at a faster pace. Our relationship to others is increasingly influenced by the supreme values of a consumer society. Even though love is a stranger to the laws of debit and credit, the underlying assumption requires that our investment in this other person be 'profitable'. And this investment must produce quick returns, or we have the impression we are wasting our time. To put things bluntly, we're not getting 'a good deal' with this relationship. On

---

12 'Géopolitique du chaos,' talk by Ignacio Ramonet during the Quebec Book Fair, 1998.

this topic, the popular science writer and actor Jacques Languirand quite rightly claims that couples today have become a 'sort of SMB.'[13]

Personal profit has nothing to do with the requirements of transformation, spontaneity and fortuitousness that synchronicity brings into our lives. With relational synchronicity, individual needs take second place, after collective necessities. This change may imply personal sacrifices. Who will enter our lives? Who will transform us? Even though we think we are in complete control here, collective necessities seem to be guiding this mysterious chemistry of personal encounters.

Hitting it off

There are of course several types of encounters, and each one will not have the same effect on every individual. A synchronistic encounter eludes the will of the ego; it is subordinated to another type of action. It is only when the psyche makes itself available that this type of encounter is most likely to occur. 'Hitting it off' with someone may therefore have something to do with the 'chemistry' of our interpersonal transformations. As Michel Tournier suggests in his preface to the French translation of *Elective Affinities*, this is probably one of Goethe's main ideas about love, i.e. 'nature obeys the same laws, and there are inevitable correspondences between the movements of molecules and those of lovers.'[14]

In biological systems, molecules may engage in a catalytic process that favors certain chemical reactions over others. By the same token, why not consider certain individuals as catalysts, setting off psychic reactions that transform the lives of other individuals?

'Catalytic' encounters may help us feel more ourselves. In particular, they may allow us to transform ourselves, and reveal undreamed of facets of our personality. In order to discover what we don't know about ourselves, though, we need to make ourselves receptive to the gratuitousness of the encounter.

We often hear people say: 'Stop searching. It's when you least expect it that it will happen to you.' This can sometimes be very frustrating. In fact, what they are really saying is that the supposedly almighty ego must at times step down, when confronted by movements from the collective unconscious, to make itself receptive to something new. The collective unconscious uses subtle signals and synchronistic timing that can lead to a significant encounter.

---

13 SMB: Small and Medium-Sized Businesses.
14 Goethe, *Les affinités électives*, Gallimard, Paris, 1954, p. 19.

We often see a lack of receptiveness to encounters in people with poor self-esteem. They repeatedly attract people that overpower them, and ignore or ward off those who are there to help them transform themselves.

This is precisely what happens to Sue, in the film *Sue Lost in Manhattan* by Israeli director Amos Kollek. The filmmaker shows us a woman who loses her job and her friends, and ends up on the streets with very poor self-esteem. She enters into relationships with men only on a sexual basis, and is repeatedly ridiculed by the people she meets. And yet, individuals come into her life 'by chance' who could change the process of destruction she has initiated. This is especially true of the psychology student, who offers Sue her support. But Sue refuses this help. This woman even takes the trouble of offering her a huge sum of money to help her improve her circumstances; this devastates Sue to the point where she vomits into a garbage can. Because Sue has been habitually self-destructive, when someone attempts to help her rebuild her life she reacts in an extreme way. While the student expects nothing in return, Sue is unable to believe and accept it.

When Sue meets a man 'by chance' who could help her put her life back together she is unsure of what to do. The man is a globetrotter—a Trickster[15] figure. Sue is attracted to him, but at the same time, is afraid and pulls out of the relationship. She tells him that he is an accident in her life, that he is not real, and this creates a distance between them. She also asks him to understand that she is afraid he will leave her; in fact, we can assume that what she really fears is transforming herself.

The man leaves on a trip to India to work for a month. On his return, Sue has become a homeless person. With no news from her, he waits in front of her apartment door for several days in a row. When she comes back to pick up her mail, she refuses to kiss him and hides from him, even though he is kind and patient with her. He even offers to take her to India with him, but she refuses this opportunity for change.

We generally close our eyes to relationships that could lead to changes in our lives. We turn our backs on these opportunities for change, often just to preserve an inadequate identity that has become familiar to us. Indeed, change often frightens us, even when we have the chance of moving from a dismal situation to something much richer. Certain individuals whom we casually encounter attract us, but our reason leads us away from them. We may regret missing an opportunity to approach

---

15 The Trickster is the archetype of movement and voyages, and is associated with transitions.

someone who has piqued our curiosity. The sum of energies built up by those missed opportunities and averted gazes will reveal all its potential in a 'love at first sight' experience. Passionate love, that we can associate with a synchronistic encounter, in a way contains all these missed encounters.

Synchronistic encounters

A synchronistic encounter will occur most often during transition periods. In this type of encounter, in which a powerful emotional content is at play, the person we encounter seems to respond to the requirements of our individuation process.

Of course, causal factors can explain why two people are attracted to one another. The biological pheromone-driven[16] dimension, the social dimension, our personal story, and our education are among the many factors that can influence our choice of a relationship. In his book *La mémoire du désir*, Michel Dorais explains this process of falling in love, and how we put a face on our desires. According to Dorais, our attraction to certain people depends on the people we have met in the past. In other words our desires are subtly shaped by our past encounters, for example a childhood friend, a friend of the family, or any other encounter that has left an unconscious imprint.

There is no need to dwell on these well known causal factors. I am simply proposing the notion of new 'acausal' avenues in order to understand the phenomenon of interpersonal attractions. Much has been written about the causes underlying our choice of a partner, and about the relationship itself, but little has been said about the finality or meaning of these choices. Collective forces obviously bring two people together to reproduce and so insure the survival of the species but reproduction is not the principal reason for entering into a relationship. Certain relationships may have been motivated by other reasons. For example, in an expanded version of a love relationship, an individual could 'give birth' to a major project that was dormant and was just waiting to emerge, or help to develop ideas that will influence future communities. Collective forces may also operate in a global perspective, bringing two individual

---

16 Substance secreted to identify partners for mating. In humans, their effect is deeply buried in the unconscious, since the sense of smell is the least developed of our senses. In ants, pheromones can play several roles, including guiding ants towards food sources. When a source is found, the ant will secrete this substance that is picked up by other ants in the colony.

parts together to ensure the survival of the species, but also the vitality of the collective soul.

Little has been written about the nature of encounters and their timing. This is where synchronicity can offer a few points to ponder. What are the mysterious messages revealed by the collective unconscious when such and such a person is brought into our conscious realm at a particular time in our life? As Alberoni explains, this encounter 'is a moment of intense joy, a time of life when we understand the world and ourselves better, when we sense that the other is helping us follow the right path.[17]

Catherine's Voyage

In a synchronistic encounter, following the right path may often involve giving up a true relationship to incorporate the symbolic dimension in our lives. Synchronistic encounters are somewhat like a star whose lifespan is inversely proportional to its brightness. In reality, this type of highly symbolic encounter cannot be pursued over a long period of time without some difficulty. The people who have the greatest symbolic impact on our lives are not always those with whom we live. They open doors for us but it is rare that we cross those thresholds in their company. Just like the visitor who enters and exits without warning, these people enter and exit our life in a mysterious way, and they often leave us without reason. That is when we need to consider the symbolic scope of these relationships and challenge our natural tendency to maintain the euphoric state provided by these encounters. Passionate love is probably the most potent means of altering consciousness. Somewhat like alcohol and drugs, we feel the need to live intense experiences that are sometimes destructive, but that unconsciously aim to transform us. It is not unusual to experience something similar in a passionate encounter, but this state cannot be maintained indefinitely.

A synchronistic encounter can sometimes be experienced head on, as long as the individual can come to terms with the overpowering projections associated with this type of encounter. But most of the time, this encounter is experienced in a symptomatic way, as we will see in the section dealing with symptomatic relationships and impossible love. In those cases, the individual is 'hooked' to the other person, while the latter has more of a symbolic impact on his or her life. That is when the symbol becomes a symptom and the individual feels he or she is experiencing

17 Francesco Alberoni, *L'Amicizia*, Garzanti, Milan, 1984.

'heaven and hell,'[18] like an endless voyage between the gods and the demons. This fact is very well illustrated by the story of Catherine.

It was during convocation that Catherine, a single woman in her early thirties who had completed a doctorate, met the person who was to become her lover. As she told me her story, she insisted on saying that she was not religious, that she was very rational and not generally superstitious.

Two days before the ceremony, she attended the theater to see a play entitled Mustafa Farek (the title has been changed to protect the identity of this client). At convocation, Catherine noticed that the master of ceremonies ended the ceremony without respecting the alphabetical order of presentation, conferring the last degree to a certain 'Mustafa Farelk'. A single letter distinguished the two names. Catherine was intrigued by the coincidence; intuitively, she told herself the man she saw briefly at the ceremony could not possibly experience the same fate as the character in the play. A small reception was held after the ceremony but she met no one and then left. She decided to go to her favorite restaurant, located in another part of town. She sat down, started eating, and was intrigued by the arrival of a man she found very attractive. She noticed that, strangely enough, this man was wearing a badge from the ceremony. She then went over to speak to him, only to discover—to her astonishment!—that this was Mustafa Farelk, the man who had just received his degree! They exchanged a few words and their business cards, and then decided to call each other.

It turned out that Mustafa Farelk lived in a city where Catherine was scheduled to give a talk on the following weekend. The two met up and started seeing each other. However, Mustafa made it clear from the outset hat he did not want to marry nor get engaged since he was planning to return to his homeland of Morocco. The fact that this was a long-distance affair enhanced the passionate and projective nature of the relationship.

On her birthday, Catherine heard about a two-year old baby who had accidentally died in her area. A few weeks later, her best friend Paul also died. Since Paul had been her first true love and she had known him for twenty-two years, she was very

---

18 This expression was coined by Jan Bauer to describe impossible love.

stricken by this loss. The atmosphere surrounding her relationship with Mustafa was laden with themes of break-up and death. A few months later, Mustafa left Quebec to return to Morocco, and Catherine experienced this separation as another death.

At the end of the year, completely by chance, the parents of the baby who had died came to consult her. Catherine started a grieving therapy with them but without verifying if they could afford such a therapy.

During the summer, she received an invitation from Mustafa: he wanted her to meet him in Morocco for a vacation. At the same time, she received payment in the mail for the therapy she had conducted with the family in mourning. As the amount was the same as the price of the plane ticket to Morocco, Catherine surmised that she was destined to join up with her lover.

From here on in, the intricacies of synchronicity need to be examined closely. The relationship went on for a time but it was especially difficult for Catherine. She was trying to read the signs that would confirm that their relationship would continue but at the same time it was becoming increasingly complicated. In fact, the differentiation of the projection had already taken place when Catherine had told herself intuitively that the man in the play and the man in reality would not have the same kind of destiny. In other words, the unconscious was already expressing what was at stake in the upcoming relationship: the need to distinguish between the symbolic representation associated with the character in the play and the man who did not want to enter into a lasting relationship. Moreover, Mustafa had always told her that marriage was out of the question. The coincidence concerning the price of the plane ticket was therefore a literal interpretation: this relationship was a ticket to transformation.

A synchronistic event is not a 'sign' telling us to do something, like a traffic light that signals when we can cross the street. Synchronicity is rather a set of symbols and does not always imply a literal response to the impulse it creates. The meaning of a synchronistic symbol is therefore not well determined formally. It is fleshed out through the experience resulting from the encounter, in conjunction with the unconscious issue in the process of resolving itself. The meaning of a symbol prompts us to act, to question ourselves

and choose a direction, <u>without, however, showing us the</u>
<u>destination or the place where the answer can be found.</u>)

Catherine was very attracted to Arab culture, oriental
dance and theater. This woman, who had given up her
entire life to her scientific career, was perhaps being
prompted, thanks to this man from another culture, into
a transformation and a questioning of her values.

She decided to go and visit him in the hopes that they would
marry. She even put her house up for sale before meeting with
him. In fact, she spent a few days in a hotel in Morocco where
their relationship started up again. In the end she was forced to
return home when Mustafa reminded her that he still did not
have any intention of marrying her. Soon after her return, she
was very upset to learn that he had married another woman.

The meaning of a synchronistic encounter is sometimes difficult
to perceive when our desires are very intense. But in Catherine's case,
several elements lead us to believe that the encounter was associated with
transformations that this woman was undertaking in her own life. The
encounter with Mustafa therefore had a symbolic value. Remember that
many of her coincidences centered on the theme of death, especially the
initial coincidence concerning the intuitive and artistic world that she
had left behind to advance her scientific (rational) career. The strong
attraction—indeed, the fascination—exerted on her by this stranger also
points to the special emotional power felt by someone who is experiencing synchronicity. All this happened during a time of transition, namely
when she received her doctorate.

A synchronistic encounter that is capable of transforming us in a
radical way can occur at a time when psychic transformation is needed,
a period that does not happen often in one lifetime. Nevertheless, some
people may experience many synchronistic phenomena while others
never have such experiences. As Alberoni so aptly puts it: 'Like any radical transformation process, the authentic experience of falling in love will
happen to any individual only a few times in life; and to certain people,
never at all.'[19]

To identify a synchronistic encounter, the same criteria apply as
for synchronicity, i.e. the encounter must strongly reflect an inner state

19 Francesco Alberoni, *Falling in Love*, Random House, New York, 1984, p.
170.

through external means. This state is made up of many coincidences that are charged with meaning—a powerful emotional energy that sometimes takes years to go away, if it goes away at all. This encounter is evidence of underlying transformations in our personality that are expressed, for example, through the development of new interests, in new cultures, new musical or literary tastes, new activities, etc. Note that it is often during this type of encounter that we come in contact with works of art and authors that will influence us throughout our lives. Finally, these encounters occur during times of transition, questioning and uncertainty. The synchronistic encounter is a sort of chaotic yawn, a reaching out towards another person, in which the psyche inhales oxygen while taking along with it a whole host of promises of awakening. This awakening, however, will very often take place alone...

Symbolic micro-processes

Relational synchronicity does not only apply to a passionate encounter of the type seen above. There are also synchronicities that lead us more gently to approach certain individuals to engage in a relationship that is less passionate and can extend over a longer period of time. I call this subtler phenomenon: symbolic micro-processes. Symbolic micro-processes are much more frequent than synchronistic encounters, but require time and intuition to sort out their meaning and direction. It is as if the unconscious was preparing these encounters for us far in advance. To illustrate this idea, here is an experience that one of my friends related to me.

> *For Brigitte, the night of December 31, 1999, was the starting point of a series of coincidences, centered on the theme of blindness; coincidences that led her to meet someone who transformed her life. Initially, at a party held at her home, one of her friends arrived with a new boyfriend who was blind. Disillusioned by love, Brigitte had definitely 'given up' on men, but she was intrigued by this couple. She was surprised to find herself saying that this type of relationship was probably going to happen to her. Following this, several small coincidences occurred that centered on this theme. At the time these coincidences only amused her, nothing more.*

> *Several months later, an electrical problem in Brigitte's apartment caused a power shortage and she experienced a blackout. She*

*called the landlord to fix the problem and he brought along
his assistant, Christian, a visually impaired electrician.*

*Amused by this coincidence, she realized what it was like to be 'in
the dark' just like this stranger. The electrician made the repairs
himself with the help of the landlord, who gave him directions,
and power was restored. Fascinated by this feat of resourcefulness,
Brigitte wanted to get to know Christian better and asked him
for his phone number. She called him from time to time to talk.*

*As the relationship deepened, Brigitte discovered that she
was in love with Christian, a feeling that she now associated
with the strange forewarning she received on the night of
December 31, 1999. It was as if the unconscious, several
months beforehand, had prepared the arrival of this man
in her life, who restored the power of love for her, and
allowed her to see the world in a completely new way.*

Symbolic micro-processes are sometimes invisible to the naked eye, or can appear to be an exaggerated focus of our attention, from someone else's perspective. These symbolic messages are much more than a simple guide for our consciousness: they determine our choices and give meaning to them. When we experience them ourselves, we know intuitively that they are leading us somewhere (even though the final destination can only be revealed to us much later). Keeping a diary in which we jot down possible synchronicities, like a dream diary, can help us discover these subtle inclinations and tendencies in our life. By carefully noting the event, the effect it has on us, and the background elements related to these coincidences and encounters, we can reveal these messages from the psyche more easily. We can then locate the starting point and direction of these symbols, just like Brigitte did when she returned to the night of December 31, 1999.

In retrospect, we can observe how life synchronizes encounters that will be of such importance to us. We may think we 'wasted our time' with such and such a person, but we later realize after that this person unconsciously prepared us for an encounter with someone else, who in turn led us to meet another, and so on. It is only after meeting all these other people that we finally meet this last person, after a slow and seemingly pointless progression. Thus, what appears at first chaotic and disorderly can in the end reveal a perfectly ordered structure.

Relational synchronicity is part of a continuum that extends from a synchronistic encounter (that radically transforms our life) to symbolic micro-processes of a 'poetic' nature (that gradually transform us). These micro-processes gradually reveal the symbolic dimension of the world to us. In the case of symbolic micro-processes, the motivation or motivations that are symbolically unraveled extend over a long period of time and emerge in a less obvious way. The transformation that follows has a more subtle action, with a better chance of leading to an enduring relationship. These symbolic micro-processes are like the motifs revealed to us in dreams, and require special care. We dream every night, but we don't dream 'archetypal' dreams every night, i.e. decisive dreams interpreted here as synchronistic encounters. In the same way that we can interpret dreams on several levels, we can also interpret these messages from the unconscious on different levels.

On the threshold of the other: Synchronicities and the initial encounter

Since a typical occurrence of synchronicity is likely to be on the boundaries and in passageways of our existence, it can be easier to see when we are on the thresholds of our relationships, for example, in the first instants of an encounter with a significant other. Without directly alluding to the concept of synchronicity, Alberoni, in his book *Falling in Love*, speaks of a symbolic dimension in the first instants of a relationship.[20]

> In the ignition state of love the number of these symbols multiply like crazy. And they also embrace the world beyond the two lovers—rain, sunshine, the shapes of clouds—all these aspects and more of nature come to signify something in the past or present that is intimately connected with the person we love. They may strike us as good omens or else they may somehow signal the direction our relationship is taking or should take. These 'signs' (which take in the most casual incidents, coincidences, and combinations of events) become all the more important for us (as we read into them interpretations, invitations, denials, etc.) precisely because we never lose sight of the fact that the person we love is different from us and for this reason his or her response to us can never be considered absolutely certain nor trusted to be exactly in keeping with what we are asking for.

Jung takes a different perspective from Alberoni because he adds a transcendent dimension to the symbol, situating it outside of time and space. A symbol is not only the product of an unprovoked hallucination.

---

20 Francesco Alberoni, *Falling in Love*, Random House, New York, 1984, p.59.

The symbolic content produced by psychic tensions informs the self about a possible unraveling of this tension that has taken root in the collective unconscious. Of course, the symbol feeds on anxieties and tensions induced by the stranger, but it is also, to a certain extent, independent of scale, i.e. the symbol can contain the totality in the details of a situation, we can find the signs of an overall shape in the making. Remember that at the level of the collective unconscious, time and space are not differentiated.

We are extremely sensitive to everything that goes into the initial stage of a relationship. The first moments of an encounter will profoundly influence all that will endure in this relationship. In humans, as in all complex systems, a small cause can create huge impacts over time. It's all a question of synchronisms and the initial state, that is to say the state of the person making the encounter. We sometimes ask ourselves this: 'Why is this person with that one?' Certain 'combinations' may appear incredible. However, if we had been present at the moment of the 'initial imprint,' we would understand more clearly how small chance occurrences transform themselves into passionate love. On that subject, Kundera eloquently says: 'If love is to be unforgettable, fortuities must immediately start fluttering down to it like birds to Francis of Assisi's shoulders.'[21]

Elizabeth and the geese

The initial run of a relationship is paved with symbols. We need to pay special attention to the time and physical background of the initial encounter in a significant relationship.

Here is an example of the beginning of a relationship in which a symbolic theme pertaining to birds became apparent from the very first moments.

I met Elizabeth through a mutual friend. At first, we called each other a few times before setting up a date in a coffee shop. Since we had never seen one another, we decided to meet in front of the entrance. I arrived first and just as I saw Elizabeth coming towards me, a large flock of geese crossed the sky. Without trying to give it a definitive meaning, we find the goose symbol in Russia, Central Asia and Siberia: it represents the desired

---

21 Milan Kundera, *The Unbearable Lightness of Being*, 1984. [My translation, CA]

woman, the chosen woman. Moreover, geese are also associated with procreation and large families. Throughout the relationship that followed this first encounter, the theme of giving birth to many children was precisely a major source of friction between myself and Elizabeth, one that eventually led to our break-up.

Nevertheless we remained very good friends. During our first outing as friends, after our relationship had been transformed, we went to see a movie. As if by chance, the final scene of the film we saw that day showed a long and impressive flock of geese!

Maintenance synchronicities

When a love relationship stemming from synchronicity manages to maintain itself in a real-life situation as projections are withdrawn, it is only natural that synchronicities decrease. Remember that synchronicity occurs more generally when the psyche is under tension, or the individual is going through a transitional phase. A harmonious love relationship will therefore be the sign that the situation is unfolding normally and that the unconscious does not have to step in to guide the individuation process of the persons involved. A withdrawal of projections occurs, leading to a greater responsibility on the part of both partners. When tensions arise in the relationship, however, synchronicities may come into play to guide the partners, and in the case of an impasse, suggest meanings.

It is therefore preferable, when all is going well in a relationship, to avoid continually questioning the meaning of each and every chance event; by constantly searching for a meaningful, underlying order, we may end up creating disorder.

Exit synchronicities

As the French say: You always recognize happiness by the noise it makes when it leaves us. Indeed, it is when a loved one leaves us that we become aware of the void created and measure the magnitude of the loss. The pain is even more intense when the person we lose is idealized. 'The only paradises are those we have lost,' said Albert Camus. That is why a person who had a great importance for us suddenly takes on the status of a god when he or she disappears from our existence. At the end of a relationship, the very strong emotional energy that is released is often marked by the presence of synchronistic signs. We are no longer dealing with a real person here, but with the image we have created from this 'Other' that stems from the forces of the collective unconscious.

The images that arise when a relationship is broken off can create major tensions; the psyche delves into human history to come up with these images and motifs. The example of the bee given in the first chapter is a typical occurrence of a symbol that ends a relationship, tapping into the symbolism of the collective unconscious to bring up fundamental themes. The case of Louis is another example of this.

Louis and the tapeworm

Louis, a man in his thirties, showed up for a reading group on synchronicity with the following story:

> For several years, I lived in an intense relationship with Lea.
> During those years, I dreamed several times that Lea took
> the form of a snake and was biting my stomach. Lea was
> a very dependant woman, I found her very invasive, but
> I was unable to put an end to our relationship. One day,
> after a medical check-up, I discovered I had a tapeworm.
> This parasite affected my health in a major way. My
> relationship with Lea was peppered with continual break-ups
> and reunions. One night, following one of these break-ups
> that had been particularly painful, I evacuated the head
> of the tapeworm, and came back to a healthy state.

This 'apparition'—the head of the tapeworm—that Louis associated with the snake, coincided with the end of the relationship. He never heard from Lea again, following this synchronistic event.

Synchronicities in other types of relationships

Synchronicities do not only appear in love relationships. They also occur in work and social relationships, where creative projects—often a crucible for synchronicities—abound. For example, the writing of this book was marked by many encounters that followed the course of these mysterious chance occurrences.

> I have lunch almost every day in a café on Saint Jean Street in
> Quebec City, located halfway between my apartment and my
> office. I go there mostly to write, jot down various ideas, but also

for the milk (which is probably the coldest in town, thanks to a set of old wooden refrigerators). I have been patronizing this café for years, though I don't talk to my neighbors (as I am usually writing), and I have never been approached by strangers either.

However, one exceptional day, I met two middle-aged people—an unusual occurrence as this café is usually filled with young people. They approached me by asking if I was writing poetry. I answered that I was jotting down general ideas about psychology, without specifying the contents. We then had a discussion about psychology and as I took leave, I simply mentioned that I was president of the Jung Circle of Quebec City, and that we had regular meetings to discuss, among other things, the psychological aspects of films. A few days later, I got a call from the daughter of one of these persons, who was a researcher in Montreal preparing a television show on synchronicity. Her parents had told her I was interested in Jung and she had managed to contact me through the Jung Circle. Only then did I mention that synchronicity was precisely the topic of my research; she was thrilled by this. She asked me to take part in the show. Once again, as with the story of the filmmaker in the previous chapter, the day of the taping 'happened' to fall on the very day I was to attend a conference in Montreal. I took part in this show, as expected, with a dozen or so participants, who had all come to elaborate on the subject of chance.

I only had five minutes to explain a concept as complex as synchronicity. Towards the end of my five minutes, elsewhere in this city, a woman felt an urge to turn on her television set. She was thinking specifically about the word 'synchronicity' and about the idea of a 'man interested in Jungian thought'. My image appeared on the screen at the precise moment that I was pronouncing the word 'synchronicity'. This woman was to become a very significant friend in my life.

One year later, she called me to put me in contact with the project director at Editions de l'Homme (the publisher of the French edition of this book), the very day I had decided to sell all my belongings and take a long trip to Polynesia. This project metamorphosed into a journey just as mysterious as a trip to a foreign country would have been: the writing of this book.

Symbolic micro-processes such as these often give creative projects a boost; they make them *sail*. With a little hindsight, we can recognize the influence of a wind that has pushed us in one direction, just like a slope that we glide down to an important theme in our life. In my case, the present book imposed itself on me just as I was about to live a completely different experience. Life sometimes takes a path that orients our personal story. If we act on the coincidences that arise, the path may lead to a perfect synchronization, designed to take us in a completely unexpected direction. We always have the choice of following this lead or not. Our intuition is needed to gauge the steepness of the slope and identify the host of symbolic micro-processes that seem to be leading us in a new direction. We must be ready to let ourselves be guided—be able to let go. In Africa, there is a beautiful saying to describe our natural reluctance to let go: 'Those who paddle downstream make the crocodiles laugh'.

Freud, Jung and Nekyia

History is punctuated with these types of encounters of a symbolic nature. In the footnotes of the history of psychology, the first meeting between Jung and Freud, for example, lasted thirteen hours and was very intense. During one of the meetings that followed, a synchronicity phenomenon occurred in the form of a very loud noise from a book-shelf. Jung felt a strong compression in his rib cage and told Freud that a wooden plank would crack loudly in the room; a few minutes later, this actually happened. Of course, Freud dismissed this, but Jung replied that the noise would be heard again, and this is precisely what happened.

From a broader perspective, we can measure the importance of this symbolic relationship of a synchronistic nature, both for the two individuals involved and for the influence it was to have on a wider society. It was thanks to their relationship that they were able to introduce seminal ideas for society. In addition, it was one that completely transformed Jung's life. The development of Jung's main ideas in the wake of this significant encounter proved to be a painful process. Shortly before their break-up, the famous Swiss psychiatrist wrote a text (or more specifically a chapter) entitled 'The Sacrifice' which cost him his friendship with Freud. This chapter can be found in *The Metamorphoses and Symbols of the Libido*, published in 1912. In this text, Jung exposes his vision of the libido in terms of a psychic energy that is global and quantitative, rather than qualitative and localized as developed by Freud. The break-up that ensued was extremely difficult for Jung. In his autobiography *Memories, Dreams, Reflections,* he describes his mental state:

After my separation from Freud, a period of inner uncertainty—more so, of disorientation—began for me. I felt like I was floating, as if completely suspended, as I had not yet found my own position.[22]

Faced with the disorder and impulses of the unconscious, Jung decided to let the images flow within him instead of fighting them. In the onslaught of these visions, he almost lost his life. Indeed, after a dream, a voice told him that if he could not manage to interpret this dream, he would be better off shooting himself in the head. The people around him were worried about his health; some psychiatrists in those days even thought he was insane and wondered if Jung was trying to treat himself! But one year before his death, Jung wrote:

All my works, all my creative activity, has come from those initial fantasies and dreams which began in 1912, almost fifty years ago. Everything that I accomplished in later life was already contained in them, although at first only in the form of emotions and images. My science was the only way I had of extricating myself from that chaos.[23]

This period, that Jung called Nekyia,[24] came to represent his own experience of chaos, from which his entire work emerged. It was also during this period that Jung completed one of his most obscure writings *The Seven Sermons to the Dead*, which contains the seeds of the idea of individuation, the central concept of his theory. This text is somewhat like a hologram or fractalization of Jung's work, for it potentially contains the totality of the work to come. While it is probably Jung's most obscure text, Christine Maillard, from Strasbourg, wrote an excellent book entitled *Les sept sermons aux morts de Carl Gustav Jung: Du Plérome à l'Étoile*, in which she studies this text and shows in a subtle way how it relates to Jung's principal concepts.

Their relationship together had a deeply symbolic dimension in that it contained a transformation potential for Jung, and probably also for Freud. But, most importantly, the encounter and crisis that ensued allowed for collective knowledge to make advances. In short, certain, qualified sacrificial relationships serve to increase collective knowledge. Happily, a relationship does not necessarily have to be painful in order to produce discoveries and make society evolve.

22 Jung, *Memories, Dreams, Reflections*, Vintage Books, 1989.

23 Ibid.

24 The word Nekyia is the title of Chant XI of the *Odyssey* and refers to a descent to the realm of the dead.

The friendship between Jung and Pauli

Unlike love, friendship may allow us to transform, without completely burning ourselves in the process. When symbolic micro-processes are at work in guiding us towards a friend, the relationship may last longer and the transformation of the self will be gentler and subtler. Friendship is a combination of successful encounters, as Alberoni so aptly describes it, adding: 'A friend is an accomplice who helps us take over the world.'[25]

Synchronicity is a good example of a concept developed thanks to a very productive relationship between friends. It was elaborated over the period of a quarter of a century, following the meeting between two geniuses in their respective areas of expertise. The meeting between Jung and Wolfgang Pauli was also a decisive one, though not as flamboyant as the relationship with Freud. We now know that this friendship developed gradually and lasted over twenty-six years.

When Pauli met Jung, the physicist was going through a period of deep personal turmoil. Pauli was often prone to experiencing synchronicities. Any unexplained influence that disturbs lab equipment is indeed called a 'Pauli effect' in his honor. Strangely enough, when Pauli entered a lab, the equipment very often went out of order. Nowadays, we have a variation on this phenomenon with computers. We all know people who, unconsciously, attract 'bugs'. Often, when we look at their profile, we notice a great fear of new technologies, or a more or less unstable emotional state.

The relationship between Jung and Pauli led to the development of the concept of synchronicity. We can also assume that symbolic micro-processes led the two men to meet at decisive points in their respective careers, for the benefit of collective knowledge.

Synchronicities in therapeutic relations

Therapy, as a transformation process, can also trigger synchronicities. Indeed, during strategic moments in therapy, symbolic phenomena may sometimes occur in real life, such as the scarab beetle in Jung's office, described in the previous chapter. Marie-Louise von Franz reported the case of a psychotic patient who, at the peak of a crisis, was astonished when a light bulb exploded—a phenomenon symbolically linked to a disintegrating ego.

---

25 Francesco Alberoni, *L'Amicizia*, Garzanti, Milan, 1984.

In an article on the use of synchronicity in therapy,[26] the psychotherapist Robert Hopcke gives the following example: A man in his forties, struggling with a persistent maternal complex, was strongly resisting treatment extending over two and a half years. One day, a few minutes before the session, a blackout plunged the surrounding neighborhood into darkness. But this was an enlightening session for the client suddenly realized he was projecting his negative mother onto the therapist, in other words, he had short-circuited all attempts by Hopcke to help him. Shortly after becoming aware of this fact, power was restored.

In his book, *The Tao of Psychology: Synchronicity and the Self*, the Jungian psychiatrist Jean Shinoda Bolen reported the case of a misogynous client who had delayed consulting a therapist for a considerable length of time. Then, in a moment of despair, he finally contacted Dr. Bolen. A friend had given him the name, without telling him the doctor was female. The man made an appointment with the female psychiatrist and showed up at her office thinking he was going to consult a male psychiatrist.

Jean Bolen is originally from Japan. The man was amazed and fascinated by her—she reminded him of a Japanese woman his uncle had talked about at length when he was a boy. All of a sudden, he found himself before a woman who represented 'the only positive image of woman' he had managed to incorporate into his life experience. This allowed him to establish a trusting relationship with the psychiatrist and make progress. Moreover, the patient was also interested in Jungian thought and wanted to work with this approach. He found himself—in a synchronistic way—in therapy with the only Jungian psychiatrist in the entire state of California.

The initial contact with a therapist and the start of a therapy are often loaded with symbols that influence what follows. The therapist can get a good idea about a person's mental state by means of all that surrounds the initial therapeutic encounter: the first telephone call, the first meeting, the reason for consulting, the person recommending the therapist, and so on. Films and books encountered at the beginning of and during therapy may also convey information about future transformations—they are useful synchronistic markers.

But the synchronistic effect is not always the client's prerogative. An intriguing synchronicity occurred during my very first consultation as a psychotherapist.

---

26 Robert Hopcke, 'On the Threshold of Change: Synchronistic Events and Their Liminal Context in Analysis', *Chiron*, 1991, p. 115-132.

During my studies, I worked many hours for community organizations. I can safely say that I learned to become a psychologist, among other things, as a result of my work as a volunteer. For over ten years, I listened patiently to distressed individuals confiding their troubles to me on a crisis phone line. I also offered many free therapies for various organizations; I even developed a project to establish a free therapy center for people with low incomes. In this respect, at the start of my career as a therapist, I had a special relationship to money and therapy, and was probably underestimating myself a great deal.

During my very first paid consultation, I was very
uneasy. I considered myself almost a 'thief' making
people pay when I had so little experience. But the
following anecdote allowed me to recognize the symbolic
dimension of money in therapy and in my life.

My first client, surprisingly an eighty-year-old woman, came to
see me to help her settle a dispute over the management of her
estate. The reason for consulting was financial, something to
which I was particularly sensitive. What's more, an issue over an
inheritance had also led to a dispute in my own family history,
and was being played out again in this first consultation.

The eighty-year-old woman was in perfect health and completely
alert. Since she came from a remote area, more than two hours
away by car, I extended the interview. At the end of the session,
while she was paying me my first fees as a therapist, the door
of my office flew open and a man entered. I was surprised, but
mostly angry. I ordered the man out of my office, while asking
what had come over him to interrupt me in this way. He
explained to me that he had just left prison. He needed money
to go to another city. I had just received my first fees and here
comes a man from nowhere (fleeing prison?) who wants money!
In the area where I practice, there are as many psychologists
as restaurants, and I found it intriguing that he happened to
come here just when I was receiving money. If I had conducted
a one-hour interview as I normally do now, I probably would
not have met him. After I refused to give him what he wanted,
this curious visitor left as mysteriously as he had appeared…

This synchronicity, which helped me question my relationship to money in therapy, brings up a theme I will take up in Chapter 7: The archetype of the Trickster. Associated with Hermes, the Greek god of voyages and trade, the Trickster is one who disturbs the established order. He is a kind of visitor, as in the play *Le Visiteur* by Eric-Emmanuel Schmitt (see Introduction), who is closely linked to the concept of synchronicity.

Rendezvous

In summary, certain relationships may occur at decisive moments of our lives and externally symbolize our inner states and transformations. Whether through love affairs, therapeutic relations, friendships, work partnerships, or even books, films and music, the unconscious summons us to an encounter that reveals us to ourselves. The relationship to others takes on a strongly symbolic dimension. But it's not so much the other person as our relationship to the world that takes on a symbolic value.

Synchronicity's main contribution—an increasing necessity in our rational societies—is the underlying meaning that attracts two people to each other. We discover that events and persons become related to each other through causal as well as acausal factors, that is, through their significance and symbolic value.

The strange coincidences that bring people into our existence may reveal rhythmic and symbolic motifs from the collective unconscious. These motifs sometimes appear to us like movements of a chaotic symphony, but in fact they lead us gradually to discover the great unity of the universe.

Chapter 3
Cultural Synchronicity

Real authors are like water diviners. They are healers. The magnetic hand of someone who writes rests on the naked heart of the reader, lowers their fever, and changes blood into water.
Christian Bobin

We may collect together and form a group on the basis of the similarity of our illusory experiences. This is a natural root of grouping among human beings.
Donald W. Winnicott

As the sun rose, the island of Corfu gradually unveiled itself before my eyes. The boat I was traveling in had left Brindisi, Italy, the night before and was stopping over at Corfu, very early in the morning, before heading for the port of Piraiévs, Athens—my final destination. We were like a hundred or so young turtles, stretching out on the rear deck, proudly wearing our backpacks, our faces smeared with grime, after spending the night breathing in exhaust fumes from the main engines. I had always been attracted to Greece, and my early images of this mythical country became associated in my mind with this first stopover on this island of contrasts in the Adriatic Sea.

On my second trip to Corfu, several years later, I arrived on the island with the firm intention of staying there awhile. I arrived by boat late one Saturday evening. As usual, I had no hotel reservations. However, Greece is like a visit to see Grandma; you experience a deep feeling of kinship and hospitality from the people and the place. A taxi took me right to the center of the island, in Gouvia, where I found a very hospitable inn.

At the time, I was very slowly getting over a break-up that was taking time to heal, and the natural beauty of this Greek island with an Italian charm soothed me. I took full advantage of the many aromas and contrasts offered by Corfu. On the island, we could visit attractive greenery, tempting beaches and terrifying cliffs, particularly the huge cliffs of Paleokastritsa that I contemplated for days at a time without tiring.

Corfu is the legendary island of the Phoenicians, as described in the *Odyssey*, the last stop of Ulysses' return voyage to Ithaca. It was there that he hid the key of a huge treasure. But the Corfu treasure was more symbolic, as far as I was concerned. It was only a few days after my return, while watching a movie that strangely echoed what I was experiencing at the time, that I realized the symbolic importance of this trip. The main character in this movie suffered from severe depression and went to Corfu to get over a love affair. In this film, interestingly enough, it was claimed that, according to an old myth, the cliffs of Paleokastritsa, the ones I had contemplated on my return to the island, could heal a broken heart if you jumped off them!

Motifs in culture

We have probably all been comforted at some point by an author or work of art that reflected a painful experience or depressed state of mind we were experiencing. Pop singers and rock bands, for example, help teenagers build their identity. I had a friend who could not imagine her teenage years without the rock band The Cure; she associated it with the turbulent period she was going through at the time. In a way, it was a cure for her. For my part, the group The Police marked my teenage years with the record *Synchronicity*. Certain authors and works of art come into our lives at critical moments, and become the synchronistic witnesses of a healing or transformation. Moreover, certain cultural themes force themselves on us through rote repetition—when, for example, several people recommend a book or a film to us in the same week. These encounters generally occur at key periods and are synchronistic witnesses of our transformations.

An idea that is 'in the air' is an idea, book or author that influences a community at a given time. For example, very often, important discoveries are made simultaneously by several scientists, each one in a different part of the world. When this happens, it is as if its time had come; as if society as a whole needed to use this idea as a guide; as if we could not do without it, as it will influence our personal development as well as that of society.

This chapter deals with synchronistic encounters relating to books, films and music. All these cultural objects reflect aspects of our own lives and sometimes succeed in soothing us, in some cases even mending and healing deep wounds. Culture is that special place for meeting ourselves and others—a place located halfway between dream and reality, that is particularly receptive to synchronistic phenomena. These encounters with books, films, music, or works of art, can overturn and transform our life as much as real-life encounters with people.

Abraham Lincoln's life, for example, was completely transformed by a set of books that guided his career choice. When he was a young man, Lincoln was poor and was planning to take up a job as a manual laborer rather than pursuing intellectual interests. But one day, he met a complete stranger carrying a mysterious barrel. The stranger, who had nothing to eat and needed money, approached Lincoln to sell him his barrel. Lincoln had no interest in this apparently ordinary barrel, yet despite this, he offered the man his last dollar so the latter could get something to eat. Back home, Lincoln opened the barrel to discover to his surprise a complete set of Blackstone's *Commentaries on the Laws of England*. These essential law books were a sort of 'necessary synchronicity' for Lincoln. Indeed, these books piqued his interest in this discipline and provided him with an education, following which he became a lawyer, state legislator, and eventually president of the United States!

Synchronistic books

When we look back on our life, we realize that certain authors have become part of it at crucial periods. As part of my workshop on synchronicity, I suggest an exercise designed to help participants reconnect with the background setting that led to an encounter with an author. By doing this, they can discover events that have been triggered by this encounter. It then becomes possible to map out the synchronistic impact of an author or work on the subsequent unfolding of someone's life. Why does this author fascinate me? When did he or she become part of my life? How did he or she succeed in having such an impact on me? These are the types of questions we try to answer in this workshop.

Certain authors will have a very great impact, and then their influence will dwindle. Others will last a long time and continue to influence us, as do synchronistic encounters with real persons.

Culture and love relationships

Authors who have influenced us often appear as part of an intense relationship. I often ask my clients which authors and works have appeared in their lives in the course of a love relationship, or after getting over a break-up. They can generally discover symbolic echoes of their life themes within these works. Réjean Ducharme and Milan Kundera, for example, are among the most influential authors for me, and came into my life spontaneously, in the course of a passionate affair. The themes developed by Kundera, and the fusional world of Ducharme, were already part of my own life.

Books and authors can indeed become synchronistic witnesses and reflections of what we are living intimately in a relationship. For example, asking ourselves what music was playing when such and such a person came into our life can teach us something about the relationship. Works of art sometimes help consolidate and cement a relationship-in-the-making. We often fall in love with someone who is a kindred spirit. Books, music and films become secret clues on the long and dangerous road to love.

Cultural objects can play a role in any form of relationship, for example, the particularly significant friendship that developed between Jung and Richard Wilhelm with respect to the intriguing book of the *I Ching*.

The Book of Change

This book, a very important one in Jung's life, is the oldest in the Chinese tradition—the Book of Change, or *I Ching*. Jung's encounter with Richard Wilhelm was a determining factor in the knowledge about this fascinating work and also influential in reaching a wider public. Richard Wilhelm was the first European to translate the *I Ching* into German, while working as a Protestant missionary in China in 1899. He succeeded in beautifully intertwining two traditions, which are seemingly at odds with each other. He did this without trying to convert the Chinese to Christianity. 'My greatest satisfaction,' he confided to his friend Jung with humor, 'is never to have baptized any Chinese person.'[27]

Jung met Wilhelm in the early 1920s, at the end of a period of confrontation with the unconscious that had resulted in his break with Freud. It was as if the unconscious was trying to mobilize people in Jung's circle who could influence his future work. Jung was already working on Chinese wisdom on his own initiative, at a time when he was just beginning to develop his theory of synchronicity. He needed Wilhelm's translations to continue this work. This encounter was therefore very synchronistic. Jung's work on synchronicity is to a very great extent

---

27 Jung, *Memories, Dreams, Reflections*, op. cit.

---

closely related to the *I Ching* and Taoism. The Tao is associated with the idea of *direction*—a path to follow—and is at the core of synchronicity.

The special relationship between Jung and Wilhelm was as fundamental to the development of this concept as was his friendship with Pauli. Shortly before Wilhelm's death, Jung experienced a synchronistic experience that prompted him to continue his task of disseminating the *I Ching* in the Western world.

> A few weeks before his death, [as he tells us in his book *Memories, Dreams, Reflections*], after a long period without hearing from him and just before falling asleep, I was kept awake by a vision. A Chinese man was standing by my bed in a dark blue garment, clasping his hands in his sleeves. He stooped towards me as if wanting to convey a message. I knew what this message was. This vision was incredibly real: I could make out every little wrinkle on his face, and even each strand of thread in his garment.[28]

This was indeed a vision concerning his relationship with Richard Wilhelm. After this vision, Jung took an active role in disseminating the *I Ching*. He wrote a brilliant preface for the English edition, in which he discussed interesting theoretical developments concerning synchronicity.

The word *Ching* means 'the weft of a fabric, in other words, the books containing truths that, just like the weft, do not change.'[29] The word *I* means chameleon or change. In short, this is a catalogue of eternal themes from the Chinese tradition. The book expresses the following idea: the background, the weft of culture never changes, but its manifestations can vary; the universal order allows for local, tiny variations, as is apparent in the formation of a snowflake.

The *I Ching* is made up of 64 hexagrams that refer to 64 themes of ancient Chinese wisdom. It is a pool of archetypes, just like simple algorithms,[30] that become increasingly complex as they are repeated. It is in a way a cultural DNA molecule, i.e. the fundamental constants of the human soul.

---

28 Ibid.

29 Richard Wilhelm and Cary F. Baynes, *The I Ching or Book of Changes*, Princeton University Press, Princeton, NJ, 1967.

30 The word algorithm comes from the Arab mathematician al-Khuwarizmi who lived in the 8th century AD (he also invented the word algebra). This term refers to a procedure that is repeated to solve a given problem. The repetition of algorithms is at the root of fractal geometry. DNA, for example, in a way contains algorithms that repeat themselves.

There is a strange similarity between the *I Ching* and computers. Both use algorithms generated by full or broken dashes, like binary 0 and 1 signals.

Here are some examples of hexagrams:

| 1. *Ch'ien /*
The Creative | 2. *K'un /*
The Receptive | 3. *Wei Chi /*
Before
Completion |

The book is consulted as a way of accessing this wisdom. The answer is obtained by using yarrow sticks or by tossing a coin; it will appear as one of the 64 hexagrams.

This procedure comes closest to synchronicity in terms of foretelling because it does not predetermine the future. It only proposes paths that are useful to our development. Though we cannot force synchronicity, we can 'simulate' it using the book of the *I Ching*.

Jung for his part used it abundantly in his own life, and even in his consultations.

> It is true that later on, I repeated the experiment so many times
> with my patients that I am now assured that these obvious matches
> were relatively many in number. For example, let's mention the
> case of a young man who had a very strong maternal complex.
> He intended to get married and had met a young girl who
> seemed an appropriate choice. But he was uncertain and feared,
> as a result of his maternal complex, choosing someone who
> would turn out to be overpowering like his mother. I tried the
> experiment on him; the hexagram (the result) said the following:
> 'The young girl is strong. You must not marry such a girl.'[31]

We must be careful about drawing certain conclusions that may seem doubtful when taken out of context. It is by being as thorough as Jung, that synchronicity and the *I Ching* can provide interesting avenues for eliminating impasses in our lives. In short, this is a projective procedure, a backdrop on which we can project our concerns and obtain an

---

31 Jung, *Memories, Dreams, Reflections*, op. cit.

answer. All we can do with this answer, however, is interpret it symbolically, as we do in the case of certain divinatory processes.

We don't always have to draw on such ancient traditions to find a screen on which to project our questions. Nowadays, culture provides us with a fundamental surface on which to project our inner states—the movie screen.

'A friend who wants the best for you'

Films are often the reflection of collective concerns, and it is not surprising to discover universal symbols and archetypes in them. It is interesting to note that psychoanalysis was introduced at the same time as cinema, at the beginning of the 20th century. Cinema is a system of mythologies that transforms old myths and legends from bygone days. Just like any myth, these new myths can be interpreted as collective dreams. These collective dreams symbolically express the major anxieties and questionings of society. Screenwriters and the great filmmakers delve deeply into the pool of culture and bring up the great oracles of our society to consciousness. It is fascinating to observe at what point a film comes into our life and how it symbolically reaches out to us. Tell me what movie you like, and I may not tell you who you are, but I can help you find out.

I myself use film in my therapies. The big screen becomes a space on which we can project aspects of our personality as well as unconscious preoccupations. Very often, a film will enter someone's consciousness at a key moment in his or her personal development; as it reflects the concerns of the moment, it can help set off a process of transformations. This is precisely what happened to Philippe.

Philippe, nearing his forties, lived a quiet existence with his wife and daughters. He came to see me because he felt deeply dissatisfied; he attributed this to a repressed desire to write. He was working for a major computer firm at the time and his career was going very well. But his work and family duties left him no time for writing.

A few days after accepting a promotion for a very important position in California, he went to see the movie With a Friend Like Harry… *by German-born, French filmmaker Dominik Moll, for no special reason and without knowing what it was about. This film tells the story of Michel, a man in his thirties leading a peaceful existence with his wife and daughters just like my client, who has put his writing projects on hold.*

The film opens with this man stopping at a rest area on the way to his cottage where he is planning to do some repairs. In the restroom, he meets Harry, a friend from his teenage years; this friend will do all he can to make him go back to writing. Since he was a teenager, Michel had wanted to become a writer just like my client. We see Michel, obviously moved by his meeting with Harry, heading back to a life he apparently has not chosen. We get the feeling that Michel has a void he would like to fill—well symbolized by the huge hole just by his cottage.[32] His wife is constantly asking him to fill this hole, that we see throughout the film; yet he is unable to do this, that is until Harry comes around...

Harry, the man he met in the restroom, is the perfect representation of the Shadow, i.e. the person who will bring all he has repressed back to consciousness. From now on, Harry will follow Michel like his shadow. Harry also resembles the amoral character of the Trickster. He eliminates all obstacles that could prevent Michel from writing, and sets up the ideal conditions for him to get back to work. He buys him a new car with air conditioning, symbolizing the fresh air and renewal in his life. Harry will even go so far as to kill Michel's parents without him knowing about it.

According to Harry, Michel's parents have an overprotective, tiresome attitude towards their son. In fact, they are completely impervious to his wishes. They even take it upon themselves to redo the bathroom in Michel's cottage—against his wishes—and paint everything in pink.

It is precisely in that bathroom that Michel will start writing again, in a way taking advantage of the turmoil following the death of his parents. We can associate this violent death to the following symbol: killing the wishes of his parents in order to connect with his own desires, and actualize his life rather than that of his parents.

---

32 This idea was suggested by the psychoanalyst Pierre Ringuette during the radio show *Projections* dealing with this film.

However, the destructive energy of his shadow (Harry) ends up jeopardizing his entire family. In order to protect his wife and children, Michel kills his friend Harry. He then kills Harry's life companion Plum, who represents the primitive anima, the woman-object. He kills both of them and buries the two bodies at his cottage to fill in the hole. He does this in one single night, even though the hole has been there for years. When he wakes up in the morning, he is a happy man, in harmony with himself; we can safely say that he is reconciled with both his shadow and his primitive anima.

With my patient Philippe, I worked by association with this cultural synchronicity by trying to help him deepen the meaning of these symbolic characters. Thanks to this method, he was able to come closer to his desire to write. The timing of this film in his life as well as its symbolic content helped Philippe to transform himself. He realized to what extent the desires of his parents had taken over his life, just as in the character of Michel. He also remembered what his parents had always told him: 'If you travel abroad, it will kill us'. Philippe had to cut the link to his parents by 'symbolically' killing them and accepting a job in a foreign country. That is exactly what he did. 'The creative drive is first and foremost a drive that destroys something,' writes the psychoanalyst and artist Pierre Ringuette, in an essay on the creative process and the concept of interstice.[33] In order to come in contact with his own desires, Philippe had to take concrete steps and free up a space for his creativity.

Moreover, Philippe approached writing in much the same way he went about his other tasks, i.e. by establishing a 'road map' to perfection. The hole that Philippe had to fill represented a space for creative play that was at odds with his idea of work—a task and an obligation. That is how we analyzed Philippe's experiences of the shadow and the primitive anima that were unconsciously 'ordering' him.

The travel theme at the beginning of the movie, represented by the car in which there was no air to breathe, was reflected in Philippe's life. He regularly had dreams in which cars and other

---

33 Pierre Ringuette, *Quelques effleurements*, Masters Thesis submitted to the Laval University Graduate School, p. 24.

means of transportation were driving him where he did not want to go, and he was always gasping for air in these vehicles. In addition, Philippe remembered a childhood dream in which he was traveling in a bus that was going in 'wrong direction'; he felt he had to get off this vehicle to go where he really wanted to go.

We can assume that the timing of this film and its symbolic content had an effect on the transformation process that helped Philippe. The therapy simply shed light on the secret motives that the film had brought up. The time at which Philippe saw this film, shortly before leaving for California, helped trigger a process of transformations that he accomplished in his life to actualize his desire to write and go on a liberating voyage.

Raining frogs

Several people told me in a short period of time about the film *Magnolia*, by the young and very promising Paul Thomas Anderson. This film examines coincidences in a very original way. There is nothing synchronistic about the fact that several people told me about this movie since all my friends knew I am researching this topic. However, the day I saw *Magnolia* may have a synchronistic component. Indeed, although I did not know this at the time, I saw the film the day the first draft of this book was rejected. My first draft was rejected for the most part because it *went in all directions at once*. This first version was, indeed, extremely chaotic. If you are reading this book now, it is because I succeeded, with the help of several persons, to turn it into a creative and ordered chaos (I went through four rewritings to accomplish this). But the book could very well have remained unfinished after the first version.

At the time, I was able to find in *Magnolia* an inspiration and a reflection of my work that helped me persevere in the very painstaking task of writing. In this film, the events and characters take a long time to relate to each other. They apparently have nothing in common, like the ideas in the first draft of my book. But as the film progresses, an underlying order emerges and takes shape. This film becomes a painting in which everything falls into place. It is somewhat like a multitude of seemingly chaotic dots that end up creating a fractal image of a fern or, to reflect more closely the actual film content, a magnolia flower.

I came up with this book in this way, by throwing up a multitude of ideas on my screen and observing how connections and flows gradually emerged. I had used this method to compose music, starting with an array of notes and trying to make out schemes and melodies in the apparent disorder. This is what characterizes the acausal principle of synchronicity, i.e. that links without a cause or logic end up creating something as unpredictable as raining frogs, a piece of music, a book or a beautiful magnolia flower 'which blooms before the leaves come out, like a miracle of spring.'[34]

The coincidences in this film are many and varied; but the one that best illustrates synchronicity is when it starts raining frogs, precisely when all the characters are at an impasse in their lives. This illustrates synchronicity because it is a bridge between all the characters. Most importantly, though, it conveys the idea of change that occurs after a deadlock. It symbolizes the actions of a higher level communicating with a lower level. It expresses the fact that: 'When all else fails, only the impossible can happen.'[35]

Frogs are associated with regenerative, underground forces.[36] In ancient China, people imitated frogs to 'bring' rain. They painted them on bronze drums because the noise they make is like thunder and brings rain. Rain, on the other hand, is associated with regeneration. Raining frogs is therefore a regenerative rain that announces the establishment of a new order. Several traditions interpret frog songs as a signal of the awakening of nature. In this film, the characters will function on a different level following this event, which is preceded by a touching song by Aimee Mann[37] that all the characters sing.

When synchronicity occurs in our life, it is somewhat like a symbolic rain of frogs. We are in a deadlock, we feel as though nothing is possible, we let go, and suddenly a whole set of coincidences occurs from an obscure source. Events are triggered according to a special logic—the logic of meaning—that sometimes seems farfetched and odd to us. We often say, when referring to a film, that such an unlikely occurrence is 'rigged'. But when synchronicity really occurs in our life, we are overwhelmed and indeed look for the person who may be 'rigging' this (and maybe lives somewhere in our unconscious).

---

34 Quotation by Pierre Ringuette, from the radio show *Projections* dealing with the film *Magnolia*.

35 Another quotation by Pierre Ringuette, from the radio show *Projections* dealing with the film *Magnolia*.

36 Chaotic underground forces from the *Dictionnaire des symboles,* op. cit.

37 The song is called 'Wise Up'.

Synchronicity and Félix Leclerc

As with cinema, music can also give rise to astonishing synchronicities. In an article published in the journal *Psychologies* in September 1999, reporter Erik Pigani wrote about an intriguing synchronicity from the music world.

> Lise, a songwriter, told us about a particularly significant experience. While she was still a student, she decided to invest all her savings in a cabaret for singer-songwriters in Quebec City. To inaugurate the place, she invited reporters but they all told her she needed to create an event; she needed a star sponsor for her cabaret—the singer Félix Leclerc, for example. She tried to contact him, to no avail. 'It was awful. I really needed him for my opening,' remembers Lise. 'Without him, the press wouldn't come. But I didn't give up; I put my trust in life, knowing that it often responds to our fundamental needs.' That same night, the young woman suddenly felt the urge to take a ride in her car. It was a cold winter night. She got in the car and drove. All of a sudden, the car in front of her swerved off the road and hit a snow bank. Lise stopped her car; the driver got out...Of course! It was Félix Leclerc! Two weeks later, the singer performed at the opening show at Lise's cabaret.

The four elements of the definition of typical synchronicity are clearly present in this example. Lise's desire to open a cabaret and the fact that she was counting on Félix Leclerc are two subjective facts. These subjective facts coincide with an objective event through a dimension of meaning: the real-life encounter with the singer-poet. The strong emotional reaction brought about by this encounter helped trigger a transformation: the real-life creation of the cabaret. All these events came about when things were deadlocked, and stemmed from a chaotic and disturbing sequence of events, i.e. the car accident.

Alexandre's time

Among the major upheavals in life, death is often the best condenser of synchronistic events. We frequently come upon meaningful coincidences surrounding death. In the following example, death and the second movement of Beethoven's Seventh Symphony are linked in a very special way.

Alexandre was a young boy suffering from a rare disease,
Wiskott-Aldrich Syndrome, from the day he was born. It is a
genetic disease that affects male children and is characterized
by a very low level of blood platelets, severe eczema and,
most importantly, an immune system deficiency that
exposed young Alexandre to every imaginable infection.

Normally, kids with this disease live their lives completely
isolated from the outside world, and have a life expectancy
of four years. But Alexandre lived without isolation and was
able to take full advantage of the vast knowledge of culture of
his father, the Quebec writer, poet and lawyer Robert Jasmin.
Culture is perhaps what permitted Alexandre to live longer. His
father believed, with reason, that immersion in the vast store
of culture, along with medical treatment, could help Alexandre
live longer. As the ethnologist Jean Duberger once said: we find
'medications for the body in the wild, and medications for the
soul in culture'. Indeed, Alexandre lived to the age of thirteen!

As is often the case, synchronicity occurred during a transition
period. It transpired in the grief brought about by Alexandre's
death. It took the form of a repetition of the motif of the second
movement of Beethoven's Seventh Symphony. At the age of six,
Alexandre had already taken a liking to this piece. At twelve,
he said if he were to take one thing to a desert island, it would
be this symphony. At thirteen, a few weeks before he died, he
learned that the Quebec Symphony Orchestra was planning to
play 'his symphony'. At the concert, he learned to his surprise
that the piece had in other times been used as a funeral march.
Just a few weeks after 'his' concert, Alexandre, the one for whom
music was like color applied to silence,[38] *passed away.*

In the days and months that followed, the theme of the
second movement of the Seventh Symphony haunted his
father's life. Aside from the many coincidences that put him
in contact with this movement throughout his mourning
period, a particularly synchronistic incident took place.

One day, while returning from work and just as he was
riding by the cemetery where Alexandre was buried, he heard
a conversation on the radio that astounded him. A theater

---

38 Robert Jasmin, *Le temps d'Alexandre*, Éditions Papyrus, Quebec, 1989.

director was preparing to put on a play with two characters:
a deaf man with an earpiece, and his son who wanted him
to hear his first musical notes. The car driven by Alexandre's
father was still in front of the cemetery when he heard the
director mention he had chosen the second movement of
Beethoven's Seventh Symphony as the first piece, to 'open the
ears' of the deaf man. It is not necessary to explain here how
Alexandre's father reacted to this, so soon after his painful loss.

He started deepening the meaning of this synchronicity. He
suddenly felt the need to 'symbolically' pursue Alexandre's
symphony through its other movements. He interpreted
this synchronicity as life's action to bring him to perpetuate
Alexandre's memory. He was the deaf man, and this meaningful
impulse became the book Le temps d'Alexandre, *a touching*
story that lends an intriguing sense of beauty to this tragedy.
Since writing this book, Robert Jasmin's life has taken a
surprising turn. Synchronicity allowed him to 'open his ears' to
this symphony initially associated with death—a symphony that
continued beyond the second movement to pursue life's work.

The culture of the soul

As Christian Bobin suggests, artists are diviners or healers who show us
ways to find water, in a completely synchronistic way. They capture the
spirit of the moment and communicate it to the world through culture.
We borrow models and inspirations from their literature, theater, films,
music, paintings, and other genres (sculpture, dance, etc.) that reflect our
own lives at decisive moments.

The moment at which a work of art becomes part of our life represents the synchronistic factor. It is not enough to simply take note of
something and see that it corresponds to our current interests. Our selective attention and subjectivity are not sufficient to explain how this work
has appeared to us, at this precise moment in our personal and collective
history; in particular, they fail to explain how this work is associated with
a transformation in our life.

The main criticism directed at synchronicity concerns this use
of our selective attention, i.e. our desire to read signs where there are
none to read. The harshest critics are those that interpret the meaning
of a synchronistic event as a purely subjective figment of the person's

imagination. Are we not relying here on an exaggerated vision of reality that is purely individualistic and rational? We cannot be held solely and entirely responsible for this dimension of meaning that characterizes synchronicity. Of course, there is a subjective component in our interpretation of synchronistic symbols, as when we interpret symbols in a dream. But what happens when a society 'dreams' about certain themes at critical moments of its development? Why is it that, at this precise moment in history, a work of art makes its way into the compendium of cultural productions? What timing is needed at the collective level to make this happen?

We can assume here that an individual dream is unable to bring a theme into consciousness at a pivotal moment of our existence. A message from the collective unconscious suddenly knocks at the door, waking us up in real life. It uses a work of art as a mediator and prompts us to interpret it correctly, guiding us in a certain direction.

The power of an artist probably consists in tapping into the roots of collective knowledge, and growing symbolic flowers out of them that are capable of mending the major flaws in our soul. As Jung said: 'In order for our leaves to reach the sky, our roots must descend into hell'; we could add—the hell of chaos. The artist in this case is the one who holds the central role, at the heart of chaos...

Chapter 4
The Chaos of Acausality

One must have chaos in oneself in order to give birth to a dancing star.
Nietzsche

Science is born when errors, failures, and unpleasant surprises prompt us to look a little closer at reality.
René Thom

The unpredictable and the predetermined unfold together to make everything the way it is. It's how nature creates itself, on every scale, the snowflake and the snowstorm.
Tom Stoppard, *Arcadia*

I was in the boarding area of Dorval International Airport in Montreal, waiting to take a plane for San Francisco. When the time came to board, I was playing a video game on my laptop computer. I was so involved in this game that I simply did not hear the repeated messages announcing the plane's departure. The game is called Tetris, and consists in lining up geometric shapes that descend gently down the screen. It was only when a child stumbled nearby that I came back to reality; I suddenly heard the airline employee's voice desperately repeating my name throughout the departure lounge, ordering me to go immediately to the gate. That day, I held up an entire plane, messed up hundreds of agendas, and possibly changed precious minutes into financial losses—all because of a video game. I can imagine the faces of those time-pressed business people finding out that the individual running to board the plane had delayed them because of a trivial game of Tetris. Our lives are connected to each other by often insignificant details that permanently change the course of events.

When I arrived in California, an icy wind was blowing over the region. Perhaps a few butterflies in Montreal had created a disturbance to make this cold wind blow all the way to Berkeley, where I way staying. I was taking part in the ninth convention of the Society for Chaos Theory in Psychology and Life Sciences. Each year, this multidisciplinary organization welcomes physicists, doctors, biologists, psychologists, psychiatrists, mathematicians, artists, and economists to discuss their research on chaos with a very open mind.

I collaborated with this group of researchers for four years, and it was based on ideas gleaned at these conventions that my understanding of synchronicity deepened. I am conscious, though, of the dangers of making forays into another discipline, and I will therefore make the necessary transpositions in an exploratory and metaphorical perspective.

Unfortunately, metaphors are not well accepted in the scientific world, as demonstrated by the book *Impostures intellectuelles*. The authors Sokal and Bricmont vigorously condemn the current trend in the humanities that incorporates metaphors from the hard sciences. As far as I'm concerned, I believe we need to keep an open mind, and explore as many avenues as possible in order to advance our comprehension of synchronicity. In my view, metaphors represent an essential element of the current theoretical breakthroughs in the exact sciences. Though Jung and Pauli were inspired by the physics of their time, neither one was able to complete the development of synchronicity—probably the Swiss psychiatrist's boldest concept. We can ascribe this to the narrowness of views at the time, and perhaps the stranglehold of the Cartesian spirit. The assertions emitted by Cartesian minds have happily been put into a new perspective by the new sciences, including chaos theory. Unfortunately, Jung did not know about this theory, as the *butterfly effect*[39] was introduced in 1961, the year of his death.

This intertwining of chaos theory and psychology is a reaction to the theoretical and disciplinary prejudices that can exist in the sciences. It will generate, I hope, seminal work hypotheses regarding the complex issue of synchronicity.

---

39 A reference to the metaphor of the butterfly effect to explain the unpredictability of weather. 'A butterfly stirring the air today in Peking can transform storm systems next month in New York.' James Gleick, *Chaos: Making a New Science*, Penguin, New York, 2008, p. 8.

New paradigm

Synchronicity implies a major change in our world vision. It suggests that we live in a world where everything is interrelated; moreover, in this world, events can be linked through meaning, i.e. a principle of agency without causality. This acausal principle proposed by Jung and Pauli to explain synchronicity, understood as a complement to causality, is a stranger to the traditional scientific model whereby causality reigns supreme.

Causality, it is true, allows us to accurately predict many phenomena, particularly the movement of the planets, the forces of gravity, and the trajectories of comets.

In a deterministic and mechanical perspective, causes are proportional to effects; we can predict the passage of a comet several hundreds of years in advance. We are however unable to accurately predict if it will rain in our garden in the next few days. In a system of closely inter-related elements, neglecting a small detail such as the flapping of a butterfly's wings makes accurate predictions impossible. The effect of a butterfly flapping its wings builds momentum over time and quickly becomes disproportionate with respect to its initial influence. Causality as we know it works well to predict the orbit of comets in our sky, but is inadequate when it comes to accurately describing the complexity of phenomena such as the weather, the stock exchange, human destinies or synchronicity. In order to apply causality to these phenomena literally, we would have to break down all the variables and take account of their amplified effects. In the case of the weather, this would become a huge undertaking; indeed, in our calculations, we would need to take account of all butterfly wings, all airplane flights, all displacements on the surface of the earth, etc.

Despite this, we often resort to causality in almost all aspects of our existence. It reassures us, though sometimes we go too far: 'My childhood is to blame if... It's your fault if...,' etc. The word *accuse* comes from the word *cause*: to accuse is to look for a cause outside ourselves, in an effort to deny our possible influence in a situation. The representation of a world where causality is predominant is a mechanical vision of a world in which all components must be broken down and isolated in order to be studied.

As Fritjof Capra states in the most complete book of popular science on these matters, *The Web of Life*,[40] reality may not be made up of parts that are capable of being broken down into independent parts, instead it

---

40 Fritjof Capra, *The Web of Life*, First Anchor Books Editions, New York, 1996, p. 30.

could be made up of *patterns* that link together at various levels and to various degrees. To thoroughly study a complex reality, we need to look at the world in terms of probabilities and of the nature of the linking of different parts that make up the world, rather than taking phenomena separately and breaking them apart. Recent discoveries in quantum mechanics suggest this by showing that when it comes to particles, matter loses its solid structure and appears rather as a vast network of interrelations. Elementary particles do not make sense here when we try to study them individually and attempt to extract causal properties from them. With discoveries such as these, causality becomes less of an absolute principle. The relationship between events and causes is one of the many possible links between the parts that make up the universe. By following the perspective of the new science, the principle of acausality—the linking of events through meaning—can be taken seriously. As we have seen with the EPR paradox in Chapter One, quantum mechanics has demonstrated that at the quantum level, an effect can precede its cause, and particles can respond to each other over a distance of several kilometers.

This change of paradigm has a very important consequence: we will have to give up some of our certainties and abandon the illusion that we are in total control of the world. These certainties were part of the utopian world view in Newton's time. Following on from Newton's world view, the French scientist and mathematician, Pierre-Simon Laplace argued that if he had stood next to God at the moment of creation he would have been able to predict the movement of every atom into the distant future. Today, we are discovering that this dream will never come true. The universe is constantly reconfiguring itself by creating systems that relate to each other. This universe is for the most part unpredictable, creative and chaotic.

New perspectives for butterflies

It was in the 1960s that the butterfly effect was discovered, based on Edward Lorenz's work on computer-assisted weather forecasting. Lorenz realized that the smallest error of a few decimals in the calculations for weather forecasts had enormous effects if repeated many times. And as with so many important discoveries in science, this one came about 'by chance'.

> One day in the winter of 1961, wanting to examine one
> sequence at greater length, Lorenz took a shortcut. Instead
> of starting the whole run over, he started midway through.

(...) When he returned an hour later, he saw something unexpected, something that planted a seed for a new science.[41]

In fact, according to the usual causal perspective, this new execution of the program should have reproduced exactly the same results. But Lorenz discovered that in a complex system, dropping a few decimals places in a computer calculation could have unpredictable consequences over the long run, hence the term *butterfly effect*. The butterfly effect is known today as the sensitive dependence of a system on initial conditions, and it characterizes this type of complex system. This discovery allows us to understand how certain systems remain extremely sensitive to initial conditions, making them more complex and making it impossible to predict their behavior accurately over the long term.

But this apparent chaos is not random and seems to obey certain laws and patterns. With the development of fractal geometry, organizational patterns in the chaotic sequence of these systems have been discovered. After observing the behavior of these complex systems an inordinate number of times on a grand scale, patterns appear. The overall observation results reveal a source of organization that remains invisible to locally focused observations. Chaos theory now allows us to study and explore this fascinating world of complexity.

A simple complexity

One important area in the study of chaos theory is complexity. But what is complexity? The word complex comes from the Latin *complexio* which means *assembly*. The meaning of the word closely resembles to 'embrace,' or to 'contain'. Complexity refers to the very great unity of nature, and the fact that everything is inter-related depending on levels and hierarchy. Complexity cannot be broken down for study, unlike phenomena that are referred to as complicated and can be analyzed into parts. A complicated mechanical system, like a car, can very easily be dismantled and repaired. This is not the case when it comes to the functioning of weather systems, or the human soul, for example.

Chaos theory uses computer modeling to find these patterns within complexity. Modeling allows us to observe a complex system in motion. Thanks to the development of increasingly powerful computers, we can

---

41 James Gleick, *Chaos: Making a New Science*, Penguin, New York, 2008, p. 16.

now study complexity in greater detail. This study of complexity has revealed something fundamental and fascinating: *complexity requires only a few simple variables to emerge.* Any computer, whether it is used to play Tetris or control the movements of a space shuttle entering the atmosphere, is above all made up of sequences of bits (0s and 1s) that are repeated many times. The repetition of simple formulas—algorithms— is the fundamental basis of computers, complexity, and life itself. Each human being, for example, comes from a single cell that has complexified itself over time to produce the person we are today.

Chaos theory is intimately related to the development of computers. A computer is an extremely powerful tool for modeling and understanding complexity. Human beings have created microscopes to study infinitely small phenomena and telescopes to study infinitely large phenomena, and they now use computers to study the infinitely complex.

The first images of chaos—fractals

A fractal is an attempt to symbolize order emerging from chaos. It is a geometric form that is scale independent, i.e. the entire form can be retrieved, no matter what scale is used to observe the figure. It illustrates the fact that phenomena of life continually repeat themselves at different levels.

The word fractal was coined by Benoît Mandelbrot, a mathematician working with IBM's research department.

> One wintry afternoon in 1975, aware of the parallel currents
> emerging in physics, preparing his first major work for publication
> in book form, Mandelbrot decided he needed a name for his
> shapes, his dimensions, and his geometry. His son was home from
> school, and Mandelbrot found himself thumbing through the
> boy's Latin dictionary. He came across the adjective *fractus*, from
> the verb *frangere*, to break. The resonance of the main English
> cognates—fracture and fraction—seemed appropriate. Mandelbrot
> created the word (noun and adjective, English and French) fractal.[42]

A fractal is created by repeating simple mathematical formulas (algorithms) and plotting the results on a graph. This process is called iteration and is performed thousands of times; it is therefore only practically possible using computers. For Mandelbrot, this kind of geometry is much closer to the forms found in nature: 'Our sense of beauty is inspired

---

42 James Gleick, op. cit., p. 98.

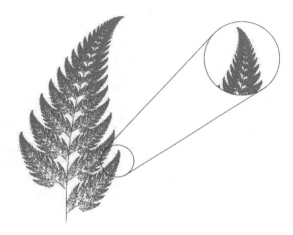

Example of a natural fractal form. We can always find the initial pattern by looking at the details (Source: Encyclopaedia Encarta)

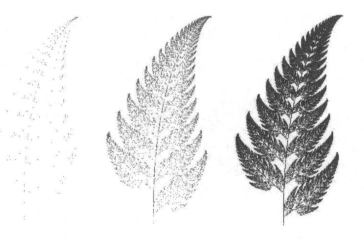

The Chaos Game: To create the form of a fern on a computer, a simple mathematical algorithm is repeated thousands of times. Predicting the exact location of the next point on the screen is impossible. And yet, this light beam always remains within the limits required to draw a fern point by point. All the essential information needed to form an image is encoded in a few simple rules. (Fractals created using the Winfract program)

by the harmonious arrangement of order and disorder, as it occurs in natural objects.'[43] Fractal geometry allows for a more 'real' representation of the forms of nature than traditional Euclidean geometry.

Repetition and human life

Repetition is at the basis of life. Our individual and collective lives are also made up of patterns that are repeated. It is therefore not surprising then to see this fractal principle shape our lives. What happens to an individual at a certain point in his or her life will impact on another level at a later time. What happens to an individual in a given society and culture will correspond to another individual in another society and so on. These repetitive experiences create complexes and archetypes and are the foundation of our psyche. They are somewhat like algorithms that are repeated throughout our personal and collective history. Thanks to consciousness, they can transform themselves through repetition, while keeping their essence—just like fractals.

Becoming aware of the mechanical repetitions of these primary patterns and giving them meaning is somewhat like introducing chaos in life's repetitive process: consciousness then becomes a form of chaos that can fool determinism and allow creativity to emerge. As Tom Stoppard illustrated in a humorous way in his play *Arcadia*, sexual attraction will always disobey Newton's law of gravitational attraction.

Strange attractors: Creative patterns in chaos

The pattern that emerges from a mechanical phenomenon, for example a pendulum movement, is generally rather simple. A pendulum is subject to frictional forces, tending towards an imaginary point located at the center of a surface, and will eventually stop on this point. In the pendulum example, the attractor that describes the dynamics is very simple and takes the form of a fixed attractor. The behavior of mechanical systems, such as a pendulum is therefore easy to predict.

In physics, there are three types of attractors. In addition to fixed point attractors, limit cycles illustrate the behavior of a pendulum that oscillates without end. The dynamics of mechanical systems can be observed using these two types of attractors, and the behavior models are easy to plot. But in the case of nonlinear complex systems such as the

---

43 Ibid, p. 117.

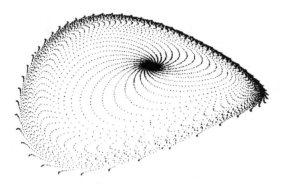

*Image of a fixed attractor. (Reproduced with
the permission of Julian C. Sprott)*

*Image of a strange attractor. (Reproduced with
the permission of Julian C. Sprott)*

weather, the economy or a fast flowing river, the dynamics and patterns are more complex, and harder to visualize and predict. These systems are open-ended, continually exchanging energy with the environment. It is only recently that we have been able to observe patterns in complex systems that hitherto appeared totally unpredictable. The attractor that models the behavior of a complex system such as a river, for example, is a fractal attractor more commonly referred to as a strange attractor.

The strange attractor is the chaos theorist's favorite tool. It is a special type of fractal that appears when the behavior of a complex system is modeled on a computer. By modeling the complex dynamics of a weather system on a computer, for example, we can discover a subtle pattern that describes the general functioning of this system. The strange attractor suggests that nature, even if it is very complex, is subject to constraints, as if disorder were channeled through patterns all based on the same underlying model. According to Gleick: 'The strange attractor lives in phase space, one of the most powerful inventions of modern science'.[44] Phase space is what allows us to change numbers into images, extracting the core information from a moving system and plotting it graphically to create a map of all its possibilities. Phase space is created artificially, for example on a computer, to model the behavior of a complex system and observe how it evolves over time.

'In theory the strange attractor could give mathematical substance to fundamental new properties of chaos. Sensitive dependence on initial conditions was one.'[45]

The strange attractor allows us to observe the boundaries that constrain the seemingly unpredictable behavior of complex systems. It allows us to keep chaos within certain limits. It tells us that on a bigger scale, an observable order emerges even though at the local level, everything appears chaotic. This effect can be seen for example when random points on a screen gradually create the image of a fern, or when atmospheric disturbances invariably produce six-point snowflakes with random variations at their center. Eddies swirling in a river are another example of this. The river always appears the same to us but it is subjected to continuous variations. A strange attractor helps us understand how a form of nature can be repeated while displaying creative variations.

Attractors and heartbeats

A heartbeat is one real-life application of this notion. Strange attractors can help us better understand the functioning of a human heart. For a long time, it was believed that a very regular, mechanical heartbeat was a good indicator of health. In fact, chaos researchers discovered that too much regularity in a heartbeat, as in many other physiological systems, leads to illness and very often death. Research led by Ary L. Goldberger, professor at the Harvard University Faculty of Medicine and co-director of the Rey Laboratory on heartbeat irregularity at Beth Israel Hospital in

---

44 James Gleick, op. cit., p. 134.
45 James Gleick, op. cit., p. 152.

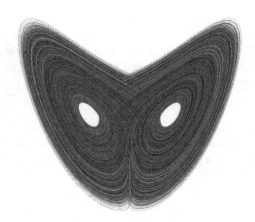

Two-dimensional image of a strange attractor created with the Winfract program. The strange attractor illustrates graphically which directions the system is most likely to take. By alternating between repetition and novelty, strange attractors are a fundamental element of the snowflake metaphor. This metaphor illustrates synchronicity and aptly describes the interplay of chance and determinism that characterizes our life and complexity. Life appears as an intricate combination of chaos and order, allowing for creativity and flexibility.

Boston, has shown that a healthy heart displays subtle irregularities that can be illustrated graphically using strange attractors. Since this discovery, subtle chaotic variations have been introduced in pacemakers to treat cardiac patients.[46]

On the opposite page, the heartbeats of two individuals have been plotted. The first illustration shows a strange attractor and is representative of the dynamics of a normal heartbeat. It shows an opening that is associated with chaotic variations. The second illustration is that of a sick heartbeat. The heartbeat is much more mechanical, which can be seen by the presence of a fixed attractor.

This principle of attractors is a very promising one for understanding most biological systems. It also appears to be a significant root to the understanding of the evolution of the human personality. The latter may evolve gradually through a creative principle of variations

---

46 Michael Bütz, *Chaos and Complexity: Implications for Psychological Theory and Practice*, Taylor and Francis, New York, 1997, p. 75-76; John Briggs and F. David Peat, *Seven Life Lessons of Chaos*, HarperCollins, New York, 2000, p. 65.

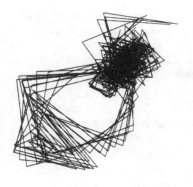

Strange attractor. (Reproduced with the permission of Dr Ary L. Goldberger)

Fixed attractor. The individual died from cardiac arrest eight days after this measurement was taken. (Reproduced with the permission of Dr Ary L. Goldberger)

like synchronicity, which regulates meaning in our lives. Synchronicity shapes our lives while leaving some room for chance, somewhat like these strange attractors.

Same difference

In the case of interpersonal encounters, the attractors metaphor illustrates the alternation between a mechanical repetition of encounters with similar types of people and a receptiveness to meeting different persons. On the one hand, we want to be reassured by attracting someone who reminds us of our personal history. On the other hand, we are fascinated by strangers; they reveal the world to us and make our personality grow. Stability and rigidity are maintained by choosing someone with similar tastes. But an open mind and growth require a foray into the unknown. Naturally, the human species generates creative variations to allow for a greater adaptation. In an evolutionary perspective, the forces of the collective unconscious drive an individual to seek out people who will help him or her make discoveries. Two movements are opposed here. We can attract someone who keeps us in a well-charted world, unconsciously and repeatedly choosing what I call 'patterners' (people unconsciously repeat their complexes in this case). This repetition of 'patterners' brings us back—in a sometimes futile way—to the known elements of our personal history, revealing an excessive taste for order and rigidity, like a heartbeat that is too regular and induces atrophy in an organism. The other movement reveals itself most clearly in encounters with the potential for making our personality evolve in a creative way, as with synchronistic encounters.

The metaphor of attractors can also be applied to a long-standing relationship. A love relationship, for example, which at the beginning is characterized by a great amount of creativity, tends to reproduce stiff patterns over time. The couple then ends up revolving around fixed attractors. That is why chaotic variations—so often dreaded in relationships— are necessary. These chaotic disturbances are like those tiny variations in the heart muscle that allow it to beat longer—just like a loving heart.

Strange attractors and synchronicity

We use the term *strange attractor* to talk about patterns in complexity that emerge in the apparent chaos of chance occurrences. In a synchronistic phenomenon, events resonate with each other and revolve around what could be called an *attractor of sense*. People, books, places, thoughts, and emotions guide us towards an unavoidable passageway. Chance events take on the form of this attractor and bring life to a necessary crossroads.

A sense attractor, which we can associate with archetypes, arises from life's repetitions and from the catalogue of the major themes of the collective unconscious and the vast network of human experience. Sense attractors are like vortices or eddies that form and take us in a certain crucial direction. They are unpredictable, they repeat themselves and they are continually moving, as clouds in the sky or eddies in a river. They allow a seemingly repetitive life process to introduce creative processes in keeping with our unique destiny.

A signature in the sand

All through our lives, we seek out a path that is our own—'our personal legend,' in the words of the author of *The Alchemist*.[47] 'Happiness is our life's quest fulfilled,' according to the ancient Greeks. What the science of complexity is teaching us with this idea of an attractor is that the forces of regulation are at work to help an organism 'find its path'. In this case, we are trying to find meaning in our lives and project our inner sense of

---

47 Paulo Coelho, *The Alchemist*, HarperCollins, New York, 1988.

---

identity outward. Since we are open to the environment and constantly exchanging information, we are ourselves a sort of strange attractor that repeats and creates itself. We have an identity that creates itself and maintains its form in a state of perpetual motion, just like a river that appears the same and at rest and yet is always different and in motion.

Our personality constantly reorganizes and transforms itself when in contact with others. We can get a pretty good idea of this by simply examining the people around us. A circle of family and friends is in a way an external reflection of what we find inside our personality. Our form, our 'personal signature' emerges through contact with others. The metaphor of the vibrating bow is interesting in this regard. When a bow is slid against the rim of a plate covered with sand, the vibrations produced leave an impression in the sand. The sand reveals an underlying order; a signature emerges, corresponding to the bow's vibrations. In visual terms, a synchronistic encounter appears to us as the soul's swift swipe of the bow, allowing our true identity to resound for all to hear.

Creative chaos

As Michel Cazenave emphasizes in this book *La synchronicité, l'âme et la science*,[48] Jung considered synchronicity to be an act of spontaneous creation. We might add a *creative order from chaos*—despite the fact that disorder is constantly increasing in the universe[49] with new forms emerging spontaneously all the time. This creative vision of chaos is not new. In most cosmological traditions, chaos has been associated with the source of all things, a potentially creative force. In the Western world, the word 'chaos' probably appeared for the first time in Hesiod's *Theogony*, around the 8th century BC: 'In the beginning, all was chaos, only emptiness, unformed matter and infinite space.' Hesiod attributes the fundamental origin of all things to chaotic forces.

Etymologically speaking, the word chaos derives from an ancient Greek verb meaning 'to gape wide open, to yawn, to open'. It is an opening, an availability for change, just as occurs in synchronicity. When nature tends to 'fall asleep' or become rigid, chaotic 'yawns' can occur.

Synchronicity occurs at critical moments, just as order emerges from chaos at specific phases. According to chaos theorists, novelty and

---

48 Michel Cazenave, *La synchronicité, l'âme et la science*, Albin Michel, Paris, 1995, p. 63.

49 A consequence of the Second Law of Thermodynamics, i.e. an increasing entropy.

creativity arise during these critical moments, somewhere between order and chaos, at the boundary of chaos. A metaphor is useful here. Imagine the events of life accumulating like grains of sand into a pile: at a critical moment the act of adding a single grain of sand can have an overall global impact causing the pile to collapse. In the same way, an apparently trivial event can have a significant bearing on our life. In this example, the grains of sand are independent of each other, just like certain events in our life seem devoid of meaning to us. However, at a certain critical moment, a single grain of sand can set off an avalanche that impacts on the entire structure. This model, developed by the Norwegian physicist Per Bak,[50] has helped explain many of the world's catastrophes, including earthquakes. According to Bak, instability and catastrophes are the inevitable and necessary characteristics of life.

This metaphor can help us understand how change emerges. Practically speaking, this is what happens in a therapeutic process: after many attempts to trigger change, a seemingly trivial event occurs. In most cases, this is what makes the difference. We may work very hard to bring about change, but this may not happen until one of these critical moments has been reached. Take the example of the beetle and Jung's many attempts to help his patient before the insect appeared. What was needed to bring about spontaneous change was a critical moment—in this case the dream of the beetle along with the real-life presence of a beetle.

A chaotic phase is often the critical point at which symbols creatively appear to induce transformations, as in synchronicity. Remember the young women who wanted to open a bar but felt unable to do so because she needed a spectacular opening act. The critical point was Félix Leclerc's accident: this allowed her to make her dream come true. Strangely enough, it was this accident that introduced new order in her life.

Dissipative structures: Order from chaos

How can order emerge from chaos? Nature naturally tends towards disorder: the Second Law of Thermodynamics indeed states that entropy increases. Surprisingly though, new forms continually emerge from this disorder.

Ilya Prigogine, Nobel Laureate in Chemistry in 1977, developed another model similar to Per Bak's 'sandpile' to understand how order emerges from chaos with his concept of dissipative structures. Dissipative

---

50 Per Bak, *How Nature Works: The Science of Self-Organised Criticality*, Copernicus Press, New York, 1996.

structures are structures that maintain their organization thanks to their relationship to the external environment. The fundamental discovery of dissipative structures is that matter can organize itself spontaneously when elements interact with one another. In human systems, driving a car is a good example of a dissipative structure. Driving on a country road, for example, gives all latitude to the driver. When a traffic jam occurs, however, the car finds itself in a larger system and becomes closely connected to the whole, i.e. the flow of traffic.

By analogy, we may sometimes have the intuition, during a synchronicity, that it is connecting us to a much larger chain of events, a deeper order whose meaning may for the moment escape us. Yet this underlying order may, in some mysterious way be attempting to reorganize our life.

Synchronicity and self-organization

In order for chaos to be creative, it must be embedded in a network of interactions. The science of chaos is intimately related to the study of networks and collective behavior in a complex network. To understand how a network becomes creative, we need to understand its 'self-catalytic' component. This word derives from the word *catalysis* meaning 'an increase in the rate of a given reaction or transformation'.

A self-catalytic network simply refers to the capability of a system to develop creative shortcuts in order to grow, as if it could call on strange attractors to help it along the way. The network of neurons in the brain is self-catalytic as it is constantly reorganizing itself using 'facilitating' neurons. In the scientific paradigm of chaos, it has been discovered that the network dynamics for several phenomena are the same at various levels. We can comprehend the dynamics of a network of neurons, ants or human beings using the same concepts. The basic idea is that creative dynamics generated by the movement of the whole induce individual parts to organize themselves—this is what chaos theorists call 'self-organization'. By organizing themselves through networks, neurons facilitate the reaction of other neurons, ants facilitate the organization of the ant colony, and humans facilitate personal and collective growth.

The right timing

For chaos to be creative, the top level must intervene in a perfectly synchronous way. William Sulis, a psychiatrist and mathematician at McMaster University in Hamilton, Ontario, has been studying collective intelligence and archetypal dynamics for many years. He has proposed the term *saliency* to describe this perfect timing at work in a network. In a symposium on synchronicity, at the convention of the Society for Chaos Theory in Psychology and Life Sciences in Philadelphia in 2000, he proposed that information that triggers change is not sufficient to create novelty in a complex network; the timing for transmitting the information is much more important. This timing, or capacity for spontaneous self-organization, is enabled when the components are brought together in a dynamic way. A complex organism that demonstrates saliency is an organism that spontaneously organizes itself by synchronizing the actions of the whole with individual behavior. This can be observed, for example, in the flight of geese.

If we observe a flock of geese, we notice they start flapping their wings at random in individual fashion before gradually synchronizing to form a group that will follow one direction in space. To optimize their performance, geese organize themselves into teams. By adopting a V formation, for example, they can improve their flight performance by 71 percent over their individual efforts. Each flap of a wing gives a boost to the goose behind, allowing the geese at the tail end to take a rest. Most importantly, they instinctively know when they must move to the front of the formation. An impulse from the whole drives one of the geese towards the tip of the V, a particularly uncomfortable position that is exposed to high winds. In a flight of geese, the impulse to struggle to the front of the formation will never be resisted by any bird; all geese know they must replace each other to rest. A human being receiving such an impulse from the whole will sometimes act differently than a goose. According to genetics expert and philosopher Albert Jacquard, a human being is sometimes 'an individual genius but a collective idiot'. People can indeed block a synchronistic impulse capable of triggering change in his life when this change seems too 'chaotic' to him.

This perfect synchronism is also present in neuron networks and insect colonies. The research of William Sulis suggests that 'meaning' in the form of an impulse from the whole is above all a question of timing in the self-organization of an interactive network. This principle harks back to the idea of meaning that arises in synchronicity.

When components organize themselves into a network, order can emerge spontaneously and form attractors; this will determine the options available and facilitate the guidance and evolution of the network in a given meaningful direction. This emerging order and meaning is similar to acausality and depends on adequate timing from the network.

We also find this concept of self-organization in the movement of sperm during fertilization. During their long voyage—the equivalent of a 6 km swim for a human being—they team up; some take positions to make way for other more capable candidates. They organize themselves to reach a destination, a common meaning—the creation of life. It is hard to explain how they communicate amongst themselves. It is certain, though, that they are very good at self-organization, heeding to a global order that drives them collectively in one direction.

Jung[51] had this idea of self-organization when he designated the Self, the archetype of meaning, as the invisible principle behind the organization of the collective unconscious, somewhat like a termite colony. Jung had observed that termites, like ants in a group, obey orders from a higher level. During synchronicity, the Self may acausally influence individuality, through the collective unconscious, in order to take us in a precise direction.

Symbolic time: *Kairos*

In ancient Greece, timing is associated with the notion of *kairos*, the right time for doing something. To be within *kairos* means to be in time with respect to the whole. *Kairos* is a timing quality, the recognition of the right time to act.

As with synchronicity, *kairos* is related to our intuition of the 'right moment,' the one we feel is appropriate for deciding on and taking action. The individual must come to perceive this intuitive time, rather than being submerged by the typical calculated pace of society that is contrary to 'kairos'. *Kairos* is an invitation to come in contact with our own internal rhythms that are closely related to collective rhythms. *Kairos* also refers to a sacred time given to us for accomplishing things, allowing us the leeway for action and inaction. But it especially refers to the idea that we are part of a vast network and that the appropriate time for pursuing our life very often depends on the intervention of a higher organizational level.

---

51 *Atom and Archetype: The Pauli/Jung Letters 1932-1958*, ed. C.A. Meier, Princeton University Press, Princeton, NJ, 2001.

Global order and collective impulse

To be sensitive to synchronicity is to feel this meaningful force, and to seize the right time to act provided by this global order. Encounters often revolve around a sense of timing for it is intuition that drives us to action and adaptation. We are attracted towards certain people, places and situations while being governed by an impulse from the collective unconscious, by something that transcends our normal boundaries. Indeed we cannot explain certain choices we make other than by invoking the strange attraction of meaning that it creates in our life story.

When we go back in time and examine the number of minute details leading to our parents or great-grandparents first meeting, we are deeply mystified. 'We win, thanks to possibilities,' said Antonine Maillet in a lecture she gave. In the same way, the chances that you are reading this book are in fact very slight when we consider the laws of probability that govern the emergence of life. And yet, you are holding this book in your hands and can grasp its meaning—at least I hope so!

More generally, consider all the chance occurrences and synchronicities within the great book of nature that led to the appearance of human beings. This idea of the contributions made by synchronicity in human evolution was proposed by Hansueli F. Etter, in his paper entitled: 'Evolution as Synchronistic Continuum.'[52] If we take a closer look, the probability of life appearing on Earth is as slight as the likelihood of synchronicity. Consequently, collective complexity, through its vast interrelations, may sometimes operate in synchronistic ways to allow for new forms to emerge in nature.

It should be noted that the accuracy of synchronizations required for humankind to emerge on Earth is equivalent to firing a one-meter arrow to Mars from the Earth and hitting the target. Zen disciples[53] will tell you the only way to hit a target is to try not to aim for it…

Acausality revisited: Linking phenomena through meaning

Linking phenomena through meaning (acausality) is at the heart of synchronicity and is gaining more and more ground in the new

---

52 Hansueli F. Etter, 'Die Evolution as synchronistisches Kontinuum', quoted in Michel Cazenave, *La synchronicité, l'âme et la science*, op. cit.

53 Herrigel, 'Le Zen dans l'art chevaleresque du tir à l'arc' in Guy Ausloos, *Compétence des familles: Temps, chaos et processus*, Erès, Paris, 1995.

conceptions of the complex world as a complement to causality. It is sometimes difficult to separate synchronicity from an anthropomorphic conception, but the new scientific principle of the whole providing an impetus for change allows us to extend its scope.

We are very much indebted to the physicist Pauli, rather than Jung, for emphasizing this link through meaning. In one of his letters to Jung on this subject, Pauli referred to Schopenhauer, who, before Jung, mentioned the possibility of chance events being linked through meaning.[54] The philosopher put forward the hypothesis that necessity underlies chance events, in the form of a force that links all things. He compared causal links to meridians forming an axis over time, and simultaneous events to concentric circles. We are chained to the ground by the past but attracted to the heavens by acausality and the collective necessities of the great history we are living. Science relates events in a straight line through their causes, while art gathers up events in a circular fashion through meaning. According to Pauli, science in the days of Schopenhauer was still immersed in classical determinism, but he was confident that with the new discoveries concerning particles, science would increasingly open itself up to this possibility of meaning as an organizing factor. This intuition coming from the winner of a Nobel prize in physics is particularly relevant for us today and reassuring when we consider the validity of a concept like synchronicity.

Patterns in the carpet

In Fez, Morocco, women draw on a long family tradition and tell the story of their ancestors by means of the patterns they weave into their carpets. Some of these women are illiterate and yet tell beautiful stories by weaving colorful patterns into their astonishing fabrics. Indeed we are all treading on an immense carpet with patterns for all to see, woven by the soul of the world. We may stubbornly decide that these patterns that emerge spontaneously are nothing but random glitches in the carpet— small errors spun by reality. But if we ignore these patterns, we are depriving ourselves of an important source of information on our past history and possible future.

The new perspectives offered by chaos and complexity theories show us that some of these patterns have meaning, a direction provided

---

54 *Atom and Archetype: The Pauli/Jung Letters 1932-1958*, op. cit. The article by Schopenhauer that Pauli suggested to Jung is 'Transcendental speculation on the apparent intentionality in the individual's destiny'.

by a higher level of organization. This level is constantly at work on our behalf, though we only become aware of this when mysterious and yet meaningful coincidences occur—our synchronicities.

Chapter 5

From Collective Complexity to Personal Complex

Everyone affects us: that's the affective domain.
Réjean Ducharme

Words are like nodes and the cosmos is woven like a garment.
Hermes Trismegistus

One day, I was walking on the beach at Wicklow, Ireland, where Saint Patrick, patron saint of the Irish, set foot for the first time. There I found a magnificent green stone in the sand. Its color reminded me of the vast Irish meadows through which I wandered, and I naively thought to myself that it may have witnessed the saint's passage. This stone, with its many varied reflections, had surely been shaped by the tumultuous waves of the Irish Sea and had a mythical appeal for me. Shortly after this trip, however, I met someone who radically changed my perception of the precious gem I thought I had discovered. This stone was in fact just a piece of broken glass from a soft drink bottle!

Just as this piece of glass was polished over and over again by the sea, the formation of our identity is a long process that is shaped by the waves of time and the unconscious. The ego, the focus of our conscious identity, is a frail construction when confronted by these forces. When the ego considers itself to be an unsinkable ship, great upheavals can occur to give it a tremendous upset. A collision with an iceberg or, more subtly, the passage of another ship can create turbulence and force us to modify our perception of ourselves and the world. Most of the time, these disturbances help our identity to mature and encourage the development of a stable and creative personality. These small, unpredictable events enter our lives somewhat like a grain of sand in a seashell. With the slow passage of time and a gradual build-up of calcium carbonate, this intruder will change into a shining pearl.

The trauma of reality

The disturbances that help shape our identity can also give rise to complexes. A complex is formed after a traumatic experience and introduces rigidity in our relationship to the world. Emotions generated by a trauma are deeply inscribed in the unconscious where they create a thematic node that will keep on influencing our existence. The most important thematic node is our identity—the ego complex—and is caused by the shock of birth. Indeed, the ego, which makes up a human personality, is also a complex. It is the most independent and differentiated of the complexes; but most importantly, it is the thematic focus of the vision we have of the world and ourselves. It is not surprising therefore that, despite the painful trauma that lies behind them, complexes are the things that characterize us. In a way, we are made up of all these fractures in our ego and we perceive the world through these cracks.

For example, a person who has been abandoned at a very early age will develop a special sensitivity to abandonment. In some cases, this may lead them against their will to seek out people likely to abandon them once again. The injury and void created by this abandonment will take on a great thematic importance in their life story. These individuals will attract people that correspond to this construction of the world and of themselves that they have created. The emotional sensitivity relating to this complex will prompt them to perceive abandonment in a tragic way. At times, this complex may take control of the ego in an almost permanent way. To better understand how a person struggling with a complex perceives the world, let's take a look at the first part of a fairy tale by Andersen: 'The Snow Queen'.

The broken mirror and its billions of pieces

This fairy tale wonderfully illustrates both fundamental elements of a complex, i.e. the traumatic break that conditions our emotional sensitivity and the particularly distorted vision of ourselves and the exterior world that follows from it.

He was a terribly bad hobgoblin, a goblin of the very wickedest sort and, in fact, he was the devil himself. One day the devil was in a very good humor because he had just finished a mirror which had this peculiar power: everything good and beautiful that was reflected in it seemed to dwindle to almost nothing at all, while everything that was worthless and ugly became most conspicuous and even uglier than before. In this mirror the loveliest landscapes looked like boiled spinach, and the very best people became hideous, or stood on their heads and had no stomachs. Their faces were distorted beyond any recognition, and if a person had a freckle it was sure to spread until it covered both nose and mouth.

[…] One day, this mirror fell to the earth, where it shattered into hundreds of millions of billions of bits, or perhaps even more. And now it caused more trouble than it did before it was broken, because some of the fragments were smaller than a grain of sand and these went flying throughout the wide world. Once they got in people's eyes they would stay there. These bits of glass distorted everything the people saw, and made them see only the bad side of things, for every little bit of glass kept the same power that the whole mirror had possessed.[55]

This fairy tale beautifully illustrates the fact that we can never access reality as it really is. It is always filtered through our inadequacies, our way of seeing things, our complexes. Complexes filter reality somewhat like the bits of broken glass of this hobgoblin who, while in a good mood, had decided to annoy humans.

Patterns that motivate us

In the previous chapter, we saw how computer programs can model reality using simple algorithms. Each one of us also models reality using his or her own life algorithms, the complexes. To put it another way, complexes are repetitive patterns that make up our emotional state. They influence and guide our existence. As long as they remain unconscious, they continue to repeat themselves mechanically and are projected on the world screen, much like a computer program.

Since we don't have direct access to our complexes, these unconscious patterns are projected outside of us. We detect their presence in the real world through the strong emotional energy they give off. What we find emotionally appealing in a person is very much related to what

---

55 *The Complete Andersen*, trans. Jean Hersholt, Heritage, New York, 1949.

we find personally moving. The other person becomes a sort of screen on which we project our complexes.

For example, we can discover a great deal about a person's identity based on what that person criticizes and what judgments he or she makes about others. Someone who looks down on artists, for example, may be harboring a similar disdain about this facet of his/her own personality.

Veronica's complex

As long as they remain unconscious, our complexes repeat themselves mechanically and dominate our life. For example, people with an intellectual inferiority complex may have all the degrees in the world and yet constantly question their personal value in the presence of people they consider superior. Curiously, life will arrange for these types of people to cross their path, people with whom they will repeat the tried and true patterns in the secret hopes of—this time, at last—overcoming their problem.

However, despite these apparently disastrous repetitions—many will unfortunately remain in this state—part of the person is seeking to open up and reach out. This is possible with the help of the collective unconscious, which synchronizes events to dismantle these emotional deadlocks and incorporate them into the self. In this respect, the Self—truly a symphony orchestra conductor for synchronicity—produces archetypal images (symbols) in dreams, but also generates real-life symbolic events (synchronicities). A synchronistic encounter can lead to creative actions that help us transform our perception of ourselves. This is what happened to Veronica, who was struggling with an inferiority complex.

Veronica, a 21-year-old woman, had it all. She was well read, dressed elegantly, and was physically very attractive. However, she felt a deep inner emptiness. Despite her great beauty and remarkable intelligence, she had an extremely poor opinion of herself. She had constructed a representation of herself and the world based on very uptight criteria—a ruthless perfectionism, a faultless rational system, very firm opinions. We could say she was revolving around an extremely mechanical fixed attractor in her perception of herself and the world. She perceived people in a similarly restricted way, judging them to be superior or inferior, especially on an intellectual level.

This complex came about, among other reasons, through a particularly abusive relationship with her father. The death of her mother when she was only four had left her in the care of her father, a reputable plastic surgeon. After the death of his wife, he had not remarried and devoted all his time to the 'good of Veronica'. So much so that he wanted to control her life. By encouraging her to become a neurosurgeon, he was practicing a very subtle form of intellectual abuse. He decreed a life 'program' for her and discouraged any spontaneous or creative actions on her part, saying that it was for her own good.

When she came to my office, she wanted to understand this deep feeling of emptiness. She hoped she would be accepted at medical school and fulfill her father's wishes, but could not deal with the situation. Her poor academic results made it clear to her that she must be a poor student.

Her relationships with men all ended in an atmosphere of intellectual warfare and all-out battle. She also perpetuated the dynamics of abuse in her love relationships. Veronica had very poor self-esteem and was unable to get men to treat her as an equal. These sometimes very brilliant but manipulative individuals were constantly belittling her. In other cases, she would fall for 'losers' that she would end up deriding.

When she started therapy, she was returning from a long trip to India and had decided to take up law. Shortly after her return, she was signing up for a course when she met Louis, a law professor, in a university hallway. The reason for the meeting was simple: they were simply discussing which courses to take. But this encounter completely changed Veronica.

Timing and initial conditions

The dimension of synchronicity of this apparently ordinary encounter has to do with the synchronistic timing and the new world vision that developed afterwards. At twenty-one years of age, Veronica was trying to free herself from her father's stranglehold and make a place for herself in the world. This need for change was reflected synchronistically in the real-life encounter with Louis.

*When he met Veronica, Louis was about to divorce after deciding
to come out about his homosexuality. The young woman fell
madly in love with him. But while he was fascinated by her,
Louis did not want to enter into a relationship with her. Veronica
was horribly disappointed and her self-esteem plummeted. She
told herself the men she esteemed were never interested in her;
she thought she* wasn't bright enough for them. *Despite this
feeling of rejection, she found Louis honest and this moved her.
She was captivated by him, without understanding why.*

*They became friends and this relationship allowed Veronica
to gauge how low her self-esteem had fallen. It was also
thanks to this man—whom she considered superior
but who did not take advantage of his position—that
Veronica's intellectual inferiority complex was stripped of
its unconscious mechanical nature. Her complex lacked the
space needed to invade her perception of herself, it lacked
the* external negative resonance *needed to operate. Louis
was unlike any of the men Veronica had met before.*

As this example shows, a seemingly trivial encounter can modify
a complex if we are in that particular in-between state—on the edge of
chaos. Veronica and Louis were precisely in a state that made them available for change and ready to cross that boundary. This allowed them to
activate the archetypes that underlay Veronica's complex, prompting a
creative change in the life of the young woman.

Collective archetypes and complexes

The emotional charge within a synchronistic encounter stems from
the collective unconscious, that realm below personal complexes where
archetypes are housed. Veronica's fascination with Louis can be explained
in part by the archetypal nature of the encounter.

Archetypes are in one sense the collective complexes of humanity.
They are the primitive roots of complexes that shape our behavior, images,
affects and thoughts. We can say that an archetype is a predisposition to
respond in a particular way to certain aspects of the world. Just as biological organs have evolved to respond optimally to the environment, the
psyche has evolved to allow an individual to respond optimally to certain
categories of experience encountered by our ancestors.

These collective patterns that underlie complexes influence our individual lives because they stem from the collective unconscious, a realm that is outside time and space. They have a creative influence to the extent that we are aware of their external manifestations, but if they remain hidden they will drive us mechanically just as complexes do. As Jung explains:

> We can perceive the specific energy of archetypes when we experience the peculiar fascination that accompanies them. They seem to hold a special spell. The same quality characterizes personal complexes, and just as personal complexes, social complexes of an archetypal nature have a history. While personal complexes never produce more than a personal bias, archetypes create myths, religions and philosophies that influence and characterize whole nations and epochs of history.[56]

There is an archetype for all universal experiences that an individual must undergo. From the beginning of humanity, human beings have a mother and a father, and must go through the rites of passage: birth, entering adult life, illness, loss, searching for a place in society, death. Fatherhood, for example, has an archetypal foundation. The real-life experience of fathering, although influenced by the archetype, will be lived by each person in a unique way, according to his own personal history and that of his parents.

Each one of these ancient experiences has left remnants in the collective unconscious, and most societies have given themselves the means to incorporate them and bring them to consciousness. However, given that Western societies offer fewer and fewer rituals for going through these rites of passage, the integration of archetypes can become a problem and generate major conflicts. Synchronicity then becomes a 'golden path' for accessing the collective unconscious and allowing us to take better stock of these archetypes.

When we personally experience these rites of passage and go through a synchronistic experience, we are more inclined to enable these archetypes. Synchronicities—in particular, synchronistic encounters—are creative experiences that need to be incorporated into our lives. They put us in contact with the wisdom of instinct; indeed, for Jung the archetype is in a way the human equivalent of an animal instinct.

In this context, archetypes are core elements of the psyche or 'psychic attractors' that will influence relations between the ego and the inner and outer world. They are sources of wisdom but also sources of conflict when

---

56 Jung, *Answer to Job*, Princeton University Press, Princeton, NJ, 1973.

our individual experience has polarized them in a negative way. Indeed, archetypes as well as complexes operate in a dual mode—positively or negatively—according to a person's experience.

Archetypes are many and varied. Among these, Jung chose the archetype of the *animus* (personification of the male nature in the female unconscious) and the *anima* (personification of the female nature in the male unconscious) to refer to the factor influencing our relation to the inner world. As for the relation of the ego to the outer world, Jung used the term *persona*, a mask that we use to establish relationships to others. He also referred to the archetype of the shadow, which is the unconscious component of the personality, what we have repressed and cannot admit in the construction of our identity.

Archetypal fields[57]

Archetypes are independent of time and space and have the Self at their center. As shown in the figure opposite, the Self, as the archetype of meaning, is somewhat like a sun attracting particular themes of existence into orbits around it. The ego is the main theme produced by the Self and will be under its influence all through life.

Archetypes are located in this field of the collective unconscious. They have a potential for structuring experience but, just like complexes, are never directly accessible to consciousness. The archetypal gravitational field can also be compared to a latent field, the force at work in crystallization. A good description of how archetypes work is to compare them with the axial system of a crystal, mentioned by Jung twice in 1946, which invisibly structures ions and molecules into a specific form. Just as a snowflake always contains six points, an archetype contains a latent structure that will deploy itself in the life of an individual at decisive moments. The distinctive characteristic of this field is to produce patterns that are independent of time and space, allowing for coincidences that go beyond what we normally conceive using those parameters. An archetype does not produce synchronicity, but it is the main organizing principle behind it. We cannot therefore predict what the outcome of an individual life will be, but we do know that each one of us will have the opportunity to experience this type of collective experience.

---

57 The idea of archetypal fields is dealt with in detail in the book by Michael Conforti, *Field, Form and Fate: Patterns in Mind and Nature*, Spring Publications, Woodstock, CT, 1999.

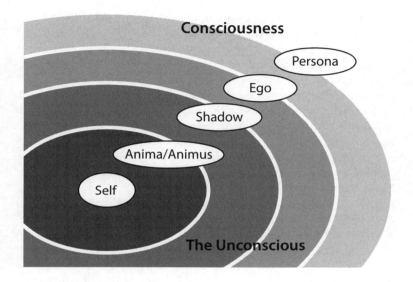

Even if all human beings face the same types of experience, none will activate archetypes twice in the same way. That is why we must distinguish between the archetype and its symbolic manifestation. As Jung indicated the archetype is a potential for representation.

> The archetypes are not determined by their content, but only by their form, and then only to a very limited degree. A primordial image is determined as to its content only when it has become conscious and is therefore filled with the material of conscious experience … The archetype in itself is empty and purely formal, nothing but a *facultas praeformandi*, a possibility of representation which is given a *priori*. The representations themselves are not inherited, only the forms.[58]

The manifestation of archetypes by means of symbols is unlimited, like snowflakes and fractals they arise out of a single essence. If this term is still confusing, it is not because of its content, which is transmitted over generations, but because of its representational potential or latent structure. It is not the person himself or herself who is meaningful in a synchronistic encounter, but the overall situation of two individuals

---

58 C.G. Jung, *The Archetypes and the Collective Unconscious*, Collected Works of C.G. Jung, vol. 9, part 1, Princeton University Press, Princeton, NJ, 1981.

who experience a coincidence or encounter together and tinge it with symbolic content from their own experience.

Before her encounter with Louis, Veronica's paternal intellectual complex was negatively tainted by the intellectual abuse she received from her father. Her relationships with men were partly conditioned by this complex and driven by a negative animus. The unconscious motives of her relationships with men included such aspects as abuse, rejection and intellectual manipulation. In other words, her relationships were based on themes from her personal story in the context of men.

Having lived with a man who earned his living by transforming people's appearance, Veronica was very much attuned to social image. Her meeting with Louis, a renowned law professor, also activated her persona, or social mask. Just as Veronica was getting ready to take her place in the world, the persona—a theatrical mask resonating with the voice of ancient Greek theatre—became active. She saw in this man the successful life she secretly wished to live herself.

In any type of relationship, but especially in a synchronistic encounter, a field activates the latent motives of our complexes and archetypes. Both persons 'enter into orbit' together according to the principles of attraction, with specific dynamics and meanings based on the archetypes that are activated. It can often be surprising to observe the particular mood and setting of our relationships, as if each relationship had its own colors, themes and dynamics. When these themes are unconscious, however, the orbit may turn out to be the mechanical form of a fixed attractor and lack creativity.

When we become conscious of this archetypal field (thanks to coincidences and symbols), we are gradually able to activate the creativity of a meaningful attractor. It is as if consciousness was inducing subtle chaotic variations that can transform these fixed and repetitive motives into moving and creative ones.

Veronica's paternal intellectual complex was transformed during her relationship with Louis and through therapy (awareness of the dynamics surrounding the complex). Louis was very respectful of Veronica and did not enter into the dynamics of abuse. He took her on as an assistant and watched over her as a father should. The manifestation of the archetype underlying the complex—the animus—was able to polarize itself in a positive way with Louis. Louis and Veronica continued to see each other as friends and professional colleagues and the projections gradually diminished.

Veronica gained confidence in herself, stopped getting bogged down in abusive relationships and found a sophisticated companion who became her partner. Her reality now included newly revised archetypes that had attracted this man into her life. The animus now had a guiding role to play, and the persona became a support for her own voice in her future life as a lawyer.

For his part, Louis came out more openly about his homosexuality and transformed the image he had of women before meeting Veronica. We can say that this encounter allowed him to integrate his shadow and anima.

It would be wrong to believe that, following her relationship with Louis, Veronica is now immunized against abuse and the horrors of her negative complex. Nevertheless, by taking advantage of this well synchronized encounter and raising the supporting archetypes to consciousness, she is less vulnerable to the ups and downs of her unconscious and can rely on the positive energy emanating from archetypes.

It is of course mysterious to observe how a negative complex can be modified, by taking a creative turn through an encounter with someone. In the previous example, the fact that the relationship between Veronica and Louis was not a sexual one probably helped develop these archetypal forms in an imaginary setting. In other words, Veronica and Louis did not become the victims of a manipulative unconscious in a real-life drama. The perfect synchronization between the need for inner change in our two protagonists and outside events helped bring about a mysterious and synchronistic transformation. Veronica's attitude of *acceptance and sacrifice* with respect to this relationship probably allowed her to access the symbolic and archetypal dimension of this experience. This encounter showed her a way out but she had to go it alone, without the man she desired. In turn, this led her to another man who now shares her life.

Change in therapy is mysterious. A change brought about by an encounter with someone is equally mysterious. 'When the student is ready, the master appears,' goes the Chinese saying.

The main archetype behind this perfect timing, the one that controls synchronicity and the major identity transformations, is the archetype of the Self—the hub of the overall psyche. In a way, it is in charge of timing the activation of these archetypes that constitute the important encounters of our life. The archetype of meaning is the central archetype that guides the individuation process, i.e. the activation of the latent potential in all of us. It could be compared to the psychological DNA of our development and contains in a bud all our life's potential. In this way it is responsible for the precision timing of the encounters that occur to help us grow psychologically.

Though by no means a requirement, these synchronistic encounters are not unusual during adolescence, in the transition to adult life, when we must make a place for ourselves in the world and choose a life companion. The archetypes of persona and animus/anima are more easily activated and projected onto another person in order to be incorporated into the personality.

Middle age is also a key period of activation, as we can see from Louis' example. This is the time when we come in contact with the Shadow. This period favors synchronistic encounters that help us integrate the strongly repressed aspects of our personality. For example, the painful rift between Jung and Freud occurred when Jung was in his forties, and coincided with his famous descent into the unconscious and confrontation with the Shadow.

There are infinitely many possibilities of combining events in our personal and collective histories. Statistically speaking, there are dozens of people we may encounter. However, only some of them are 'picked up' by the 'orbit' of an archetypal field to activate a latent form we need to integrate in our personality. These transformations sometimes appear to us as a meaningful coincidence or perfectly synchronistic—yet deeply troubling—encounter. Something is trying to express itself here and it takes the form of an encounter.

Though our encounters are due to chance, they follow the forms and rhythms of archetypes. It is as if life were constantly playing dice that are controlled by the archetype of meaning. These dice function through, and are influenced by, a central entity that becomes manifest in the form of synchronistic encounters. While these encounters may be beyond our comprehension, the coincidences involved may be worthy of the best movie scripts.

During a synchronistic event, two main archetypes are present: the archetype of the Self, and the archetype of Mercury, Hermes or the Trickster. They manifest themselves in several forms as with any other archetype, but their presence can be revealed to us through their specific dynamics associated with movement and transformation. They will make up the main themes of the next two chapters.

In the face of our fixed complexes and repetitions in our life, archetypes—when we become conscious of them—are creative attractors, meaningful attractors that help in a mysteriously acausal way to modify the 'logic' or events of our life. They are used to guide major transformations in our lives and add a creative touch to the repetitive motives of our existence.

Chapter 6

The Meaning of Transformation

While winter
Rests in my belly
And whitens my blood
Little by little, I extenuate death.
    Isabelle Forest

In the same way,
In the desert, the forces of the soul and the passions must exist in their
purest form, in a brilliant transparency. They have all immensity in
which to unfold.
    Roland Bourneuf

The desert symbolizes the difficult passage from one state to another, from a place of suffering to the Promised Land. This vast expanse of sand associated with transformations has always exerted a strange fascination on me, and I have vivid memories of my first expedition to the Sahara Desert. After several hours on the road and three flat tires, I was at last able to see the majestic dunes of the Sahara Desert, through the window of the red pickup truck that was taking me to the epitome of dunes: Merzouga, Morocco. Sand, sand, and still more sand—a paradoxical symbol of immutability and change. The wind blows over these huge golden mountains and establishes its ordered realm, leaving its distinctive signature behind. Patterns form in the midst of simoon and sirocco winds. Then there is the sunrise with its contrasts and shadows, adding its own touch to the landscape.

In the desert, as the day progresses and the sun rises high above our heads, the heat is so intense that we are forced to stop and find some shade.

When night has fallen, shadows are everywhere, but this is when travel becomes possible. My most vivid memory of my experience in the desert relates specifically to this time of day, while waiting for the moon to rise above the dunes. This simple waiting ritual practiced by Berbers in absolute silence was an unforgettable experience. At midnight, we were thirsty and the reflection of the moon over the dunes reached us like a long milky way splashed onto a huge honey-golden carpet.

This carpet of light as well as the stars become reference points. The best time to travel in the desert, explained Yosef, the Berber who shared these moments with me, is at night, at dusk, and at dawn. That is when you have a chance to find a source of water to quench your thirst. I thought about these periods of darkness and the difficult transitions that come with them. The important passages such as adolescence and midlife are periods in which we are searching intensively for signs to give a meaning to our life.

The meaning of our story

To look for a meaning is to start seeking a well, a source of water, as we do when we travel in the desert. To look for a meaning is also to look for the delicate silk thread that weaves over and mends the major inadequacies in our life. As Kundera writes, we are constantly looking for signs that link us to our story.

> Do stories, apart from happening, being, have something to say? For all my skepticism, some trace of irrational superstition did survive in me, the strange conviction, for example, that everything in life that happens to me also has a sense, that it means something, that life speaks to us about itself through its story, that it gradually reveals a secret, that it takes the form of a rebus whose message must be deciphered, that the stories we live comprise the mythology of our lives and in that mythology lies the key to truth and mystery. Is it an illusion? Possibly, even probably, but I can't rid myself of the need continually to *decipher* my own life..[59]

The Self and synchronicity

The need for meaning and coherence in our personal myths probably comes from the Self. Among the archetypes, the Self is, according to Jung,

---

59 Milan Kundera, *The Joke*, 1993. [My translation CA]

the central archetype, the organizing principle—the one that guides the process that turns us into increasingly complete persons, namely individuation. It is in fact a unifying force whose role is to harmonize, bring together and intertwine all the conscious and unconscious components of our personality, turning them into a creative whole. It is the archetype of meaning and of wholeness and is more extensive than the self. Jung wrote: 'The self is not only the center, but also the whole circumference which embraces both the conscious and the unconscious; it is the center of this totality, just as the ego is the center of consciousness.'[60] He added: 'The Self is our life's goal, for it is the expression of that fateful combination we call an individual.'[61] It is therefore the goal but also the means by which individuation occurs. It is both the destination and the voyage.

The Self is the unconscious center with which the ego must deal throughout the individuation process. It is the main generator of symbols in the psyche that appear in dreams and in the form of synchronicities in real-life situations.

Fractals and mandalas

The Self is symbolically represented by a circle or a mandala. For the Tibetan Buddhist, a mandala is an imaginary palace that he contemplates during meditation. Each one of its patterns has a meaning and helps the meditator deepen one aspect of Tibetan wisdom. Mandalas are generally made of paper, fabric or sand. They come in an infinite variety of forms and several spiritual traditions use this figure. The Navajos of New Mexico, for example, use sand mandalas of various colors. It can take several weeks to build a mandala that is ritually destroyed after contemplation.

According to Jung,[62] the mandala can appear spontaneously in the form of dreams during the critical phases of life—just like synchronicities. Mandalas are very important for understanding the creative drive of symbols in periods of disarray or chaos. Jung says on this topic: 'We know from experience that the protective circle, the mandala is the traditional antidote to chaotic states of mind.'[63]

60 C.G. Jung, *Psychology and Alchemy*, Collected Works of C.G. Jung, vol. 12, Princeton University Press, Princeton, NJ, 1980.

61 C.G. Jung, *Aion: Researches into the Phenomenology of the Self*, Collective Works of C.G. Jung, vol. 9, part 2, Princeton University Press, Princeton, NJ, 1980.

62 C.G. Jung, *The Archetypes and the Collective Unconscious*, op. cit.

63 Ibid.

*Painted 17th century Tibetan
'Five Deity Mandala'. Rubin
Museum of Art, New York.*

*Fractal realized by Jules J.C.M.
Ruis, Fractal Design and
Consulting Group, Holland]*

Science increasingly relies on fractal representations to identify organizational 'schemes' in complex biological systems, some of which strangely resemble mandalas. According to Vladimir Gontar, from Ben-Gurion University of the Negev,[64] Israel, certain biochemical reactions of the brain may even take the form of a mandala when modeled using fractal geometry. Mandalas created by the psyche in periods of crisis also seem to appear in the chemistry of a brain attempting to overcome an obstacle through creative adaptation.

The symmetry of a mandala highlights the importance of a permanent center around which experience revolves. The mandala[65] can also represent the wheel, an important figure in Eastern traditions. On the circumference of the wheel, for example, movement and chaos are greater; but as we move towards the center, stability increases—just as when we move nearer to the center of the Self. Local chaos therefore does not mean disorder in the overall psyche. There may be local confusion at the circumference of the ego while an overall order emanates from the center of the Self.

---

64 Vladimir Gontar, 'Theoretical Foundation of Jung's "Mandala Symbolism", based on Discrete Chaotic Dynamics of Interacting Neurons, *Discrete Dynamics in Nature and Society*, vol. 5, No 1, 2000, pp. 19-28.

65 The word *mandala* comes from the Sanskrit meaning *magic circle*.

The maze of life

The mandala also refers to the idea of the maze of life, similar to the labyrinthine corridors of a castle. Using the global perspective suggested by this figure, we can identify the dead ends that repeat themselves. The walls lining the maze of the mandala can represent the recurring complexes that shrink our vision of the world.

The symbolic hindsight suggested by the mandala (associated with the maze) helps individuals seek out the dark corners of their psyche and identify repetitions that make them go in circles. The events of our life, and more particularly the dead ends where they come to a standstill, may seem trivial to those examining them on an individual basis. They are somewhat like the points that light up at random on the screen when drawing a fractal. What defines us above all is the path we have chosen to live our life. There are no two identical paths, just like there are no two perfectly identical mandalas or snowflakes. The meaning we have given to our life when it ends will, in a way, be the unique path we have taken.

The Self, as a creative principle, functions somewhat like the teacher, played by Robin Williams, in the film *The Dead Poets Society*. He climbs on top of his desk to encourage his students to look at the world differently. Synchronicity is a manifestation of the Self and resembles the gesture of this teacher who provides us with a perspective and *raises us above the labyrinth of our life*.

For Jung, the Self is associated with the representation of God. The projection of the archetype of the Self in the form of celestial divinities is, analogically speaking, an attempt to place a mirror above ourselves in order to reflect our inner labyrinth. When a collective mirror is broken, as in Andersen's fairy tale 'The Snow Queen,' this can give rise to devastating religious bigotry (extreme forms of fundamentalism, for example). This projection, by reflecting the labyrinth, refers back to our need for meaning, coherence and transcendence generally provided to us by religion and spirituality. The mirror's distortion and the impression that the divinities are located *outside the self* constitute stages of individuation. These stages culminate in a re-appropriation of images that in the end are considered for what they are in truth: the reflection of *our inner world*.

Today, this projection can in particular be found in the huge labyrinth of the Internet—a projection of the Self in a center that is everywhere, with a circumference that is nowhere.

Finding the missing half

Symbols are produced by the Self, but what exactly are symbols? Etymologically speaking, symbols are associated with the *symbolon*, a piece of clay that is separated and then reunited in Greek mythology. At first, the *symbolon* was a coin that was cut in two, with both parts fitting into each other exactly: 'Two people each keep their half, a host and a guest, the lender and the debtor, two pilgrims, two people who will be separated for a long time... By bringing the two halves together at some point in the future, they will remember their hospitality links, their debts, their friendship.'[66]

We spend our lives looking for this missing half, i.e. we try to find a perfect fit using symbols. We go through life trying to fill this initial void and find this missing piece somewhere in the world—a quest for meaning as it were. There are many ways to fill this void and give meaning to our lives: work, relationships, art, sports, religion, spirituality, leisure activities and, in pathological cases, alcohol, drugs, Internet addictions, etc.

The symbolic function is what allows us to deal with the angst of reality. Symbols help us relate to the unknown, the void. It always stems from a tension and develops itself to stimulate our creativity, 'opening' us up to the unknown to release tension. Jung refers to the symbol as *the best expression and representation of a problem situation that is not yet apprehended by consciousness but which gathers together the various aspects of a psychic tension.*[67] The symbol sums up the state of the psyche and proposes a direction for resolving the conflict by calling on the unconscious as well as consciousness. According to Jung, the symbol proposes a direction because it is subordinated to the archetypes through the collective unconscious, a veritable well of collective experiences.[68]

Game playing and reality

How does this symbolic function for dealing with stress from the chaotic and unpredictable outside world develop itself? The British pediatrician and psychoanalyst Donald W. Winnicott[69] made a major contribution towards understanding the process by which we deal with reality, thanks

---

66 Jean Chevalier, *Dictionnaire des symboles*, Robert Laffont, Paris, 1982.

67 Elie Humbert, *Jung*, Éditions Universitaires, Paris, 1983, p. 44.

68 Jung refers to the deepest level of the unconscious (collective unconscious) as an objective—even independent—psyche.

69 Donald W. Winnicott, *Playing and Reality*, Routledge, New York, 1999.

---

to his research on symbolic functions. Winnicott revealed, through his notions of the holding environment (both physical and psychic) and transitional objects, the progress made by a child living in an all-powerful, make-believe world that will develop into an unpredictable and stressful outside world. This pediatrician spent hours and hours observing interactions between newborns and mothers to develop his theories. He developed the notion of transitional object to describe the development of the symbolic function.

When they first enter the world, children do not distinguish between the outer and inner worlds. A hungry child between birth and six months of age has the impression that food just appears according to his or her wishes, like an extension of him- or herself. At first, this perfect synchronization allows a child to perceive its 'power' in a world that it considers to be an extension of itself. This continues successfully until the day the child feels hunger without getting the satisfaction of eating. At that time, the child will experience its first break with reality. He/she will become aware of the existence of an outside world different from his/her inner world and will feel anxiety and tension that are resolved by the emergence of a symbolic function. This function emerges when the child chooses an object (i.e. a security blanket) that will act as transitional object, integrating both the outside world—through its objective reality—and inner worlds—through its reassuring emotional qualities (often, this is the mother's smell embedded in the blanket which brings back memories of satisfied needs and diminishes stress). This object will become symbolic in the sense that it unites both inner and outer aspects and relieves tensions created by the rift between the two worlds. The symbol is a link between the two worlds; it unites them.

When the child recognizes that he/she is different from another person (the mother), language skills develop—the first babblings of symbolic experience. But it is in this special place that creativity is also developed, helping the infant survive in the stressful world of 'differences'. It is in the awareness of differences that humans are distinct from animals; the symbolic and creative dimension (language, for example) is what is typically human.

This is how an intermediate zone, halfway between reality and imagination, develops, encompassing language and the entire symbolic universe. This is a kind of playground that allows us to respond creatively to life rather than being subjected to its laws. Later on, this transitional area will expand and become shared, in the form of culture, the arts, religion and spirituality. These symbolic spheres all stem from transitional processes and are necessary for dealing with the endless conflict between what is objectively perceived and what is subjectively conceived.

This zone is also that of religion, taking transitional objects to their maximum extension to the entire universe. This symbolic dimension is an abstraction of the real world that allows us to recreate it. But this abstraction can sometimes lead to religious bigotry and war, in which human beings kill each other over what in essence is a babies security blanket.

Signs and symbols

According to Jung,[70] symbols must not be confused with signs. The word we use to refer to something known is a sign, not a symbol. Jung does not consider a symbol to be something else in disguise. Of course, for him the symbol has a meaning; but it is not like something repressed that reappears in the borrowed form of a symbolic image. This image then would only be a symptom of a conflict; it would be unable to express the normal tendency of the psyche to develop its potential throughout the individuation process.

For Jung, symbols are a product stemming from the collective unconscious. The spontaneous creation of symbols by the Self allows us to unite opposing terms and tensions and is part of this natural tendency of life that seeks out the unknown and prompts us to continually surpass ourselves through creative acts. We can observe this creativity in nature, a nature that is 'always finding its way' to paraphrase Michael Crichton, author of the book behind the film *Jurassic Park*. This same force is at work in the psyche, through symbols.

The more the symbolic function becomes developed and complex in a child, the more deeply the unconscious will delve into its great pool of collective objects to come up with 'security blankets' or collective symbols able to unravel tensions and heal the major wounds of the soul. When we are attuned to the symbols and 'security blankets' that mysteriously appear in these cultural synchronicities (film, literature, theater, music, etc.), we are accessing the wisdom of the collective unconscious.

---

70 C.G. Jung and H.G. Baynes, *Psychological Types* or *The Psychology of Individuation*, Kegan Paul Trench Trubner, London, 1921. In this book, the explanation of the term *symbol* takes up the better part of the glossary (9 pages).

Making sense or finding sense

In synchronicity, we may wonder if the symbol's underlying meaning is only subjectively valid. According to Jung, at the collective unconscious level, the Self that naturally creates symbols produces meaning.

It is a significant coincidence that meaning appears to be driven by the archetype of wholeness or Self. It is as if a dialogue was momentarily established in a synchronicity between the 'director' (the Self) and the 'main character' of the story (the ego). The ego can choose to follow this impulse arising from the whole, or reject it. The ego can refuse to play its 'part'. It is the extent to which the ego responds to the symbolic impulses from the Self that determines if a life story is coherent and a personal myth accomplished. We may be tempted to play roles that are not part of our story but that are 'in the air,' and cause us to develop a kind of symptomatic myth-making that leads us astray from a meaning appropriate to our life.

Meaning is perceived in an intermediate zone, halfway between objective reality and subjectivity. It is perceived in a transitional space where symbols that unify opposing forces are deployed. The symbolic flowers of the Self grow in the space between the rational concrete and the archaic fields of the unconscious. When our consciousness is completely paved by concrete rationality, the flower—symbol or synchronicity—cannot be perceived. On the other hand, when our ego is too frail, organized meanings break down and we risk being overwhelmed by 'primitive undergrowth' from the unconscious.

The perception of synchronistic symbols is therefore a continual task of shaping the symbolic world. The awareness of the symbolic world, like the awareness of the dream world, can dwindle if we don't pay attention to it. Synchronicity suggests that rationality leave room for irrationality, in a transitional space halfway between reality and imagination.

It is never the external synchronistic event as such that holds meaning. The meaning develops gradually as the story unfolds in the way we decide to pursue our existence after a specific event. A symbol is not a predetermined sign; by contrast a red light is a determinate sign that tells us to stop. If a symbol were a sign, we could interpret it literally. A synchronistic symbol is rather a signal that guides us in life (choosing this solution, for example, rather than others). However, it is essential, that symbols not be taken at face value, as Catherine did when she believed that the money she received as payment for her therapy with the grieving family was a sign that she should buy an airplane ticket to visit Mustafa Farelk in Morocco.

Symbols are perceived in the transitional area, a place located between reality and dreams. Synchronicity is also perceived in this in-between space, a space for play and creativity that allows us to reinvent the world rather than being subjected to it. Symbols allow us to abstractly remove ourselves from the world and deal with the anguish it generates. The symbolic world can however take us dangerously far from reality.

Destructive fantasies

When faced with an unknown situation, we naturally create symbols. And when the unknown before us is a person, we project our desires and anxieties onto this person. This is so true, in fact, that often our own person and projections prevent us from even hearing what they have to say. This is exactly what happens in the film *A Pornographic Affair* by Belgian director Frederic Fonteyne. This film tells the story of a man and woman who meet through the classified ads. Both decide to see each other once a week to bring a fantasy to reality. The power of imagination is already apparent at the outset in two flashback scenes where each character reflects back on his/her story. Indeed, both characters think differently about the way they met and how often they were to meet. We never discover what their fantasy is, for that matter. This film emphasizes subjective perception and the power of fantasy in a relationship.

As time passes, the relationship becomes serious, to the point where both characters are driven against their will by circumstances that take them to the brink of a transformation. We then witness a very moving scene in which we see the couple facing each other in a restaurant. We hear their tiny inner voices revealing their secret desire that they should not part. But in fact they are going to tell each other exactly the opposite of what they are thinking. This scene illustrates how a fantasy that supports a relationship can also break it. It demonstrates that what unites us to others is sometimes based on nothing more than a *detail*. A word pronounced in an extreme situation can have enormous repercussions, just like the flap of a butterfly's wings in Peking will set off a storm in New York. In this case, the characters will not undergo a transformation and will eventually break up.

Symbol and symptom: Crossing the channel

Symbols stemming from the Self create a constant flux that persuades us to undergo transformations. The only thing that is constant and certain is change itself. The only thing we can be sure about, said Buddha, is that our life will change. But this movement that prompts change, especially in relationships with others, can break down if we reject the transformation's meaning. The non-integrated symbol then takes the form of a symptom. When the meaning we get from symbols—in dreams as well as in synchronicity—does not keep step with reality, it becomes a repetitive symptom.

Let's examine the major difference between a symbol and a symptom. A symbol is a representation based closely on experience, a direct representation of the situation we are experiencing. A symptom is rather a means of creating a distance between experience and the means to represent it. The symptom is very well illustrated by the metaphor of crossing the Channel.[71]

Let's imagine, for example, that you have always lived in England. You have never left this country and are used to left-hand side driving. Then a disaster occurs and you are forced to move to France. You take your car and cross the English Channel. On the other side, however, you insist on driving in the English manner. You are using a behavior set from your previous situation that does not take account of the channel crossing transformation. With any luck, you may be able to drive long enough to get to a restaurant and take a break from these 'drunken drivers'. You are indeed convinced that 'the other drivers' are the ones with driving problems. After your meal, you take to the wheel and smash into a truck. You are of course convinced that the truck driver is responsible for this accident.

A symptom acts somewhat like this English driver who had never left his country. He tries to operate in a register that does not take account of the current situation. When we operate in a symptomatic mode, we spend a huge amount of energy uselessly repeating our compulsions. We must therefore make a change in order to regain our potential and follow life's rhythms of transformation. To regain our feeling of intrinsic value, we must transform the slogans of our life; if we don't do this, we could pay dearly for maintaining our old ways. This is also what happens when we feel we have lost our values because we have continued with a lifestyle that we have tried to leave behind.

In our love life, we often make the mistake of entering into 'symptomatic' relationships that do not take account of our state of transformation. We try to become the other person. We are similar to one of my

---

71 Adapted from a metaphor by psychoanalyst René Roussillon concerning symptoms.

clients who at his first therapy session exclaimed after a difficult period of mourning: 'I did everything I could to make her love me.' Let's transpose this to: 'I suffered everything I could to make her love me.' Poor self-esteem is often at the heart of this type of relationship and at the heart of impossible love.

'Bad' synchronicities: Impossible love

One day, I referred a client to Jan Bauer's excellent book *Impossible Love.*[72] It turned out that I was the fourth person that week to recommend the book to him. Obviously, he ended up reading it, but this coincidence made him more attuned to the contents. In the same way, a significant coincidence that puts two people in touch with one another can also generate a greater availability for the other person.

According to Jan Bauer, in impossible love, the other person takes on a 'symbolic' value and puts us in touch with unknown and repressed aspects of our personality. According to the author, during these passionate encounters, we are led to go through *heaven and hell*. These relationships are an initiation to aspects of the self and can become symptomatic—emotionally dependent—when the projected symbolic dimension is not integrated. We are attached to something outside the self that in fact lives deep inside us.

Impossible love can also be present in the form of *compulsive repetitive encounters*, in which relationships are never possible. Unconsciously, we prevent the other person from drawing too near to us, probably to avoid reaching those aspects of ourselves that we don't want to show.

This type of encounter is 'apparently' poorly synchronized from the ego's point of view. But from the Self's perspective, it is perfectly synchronized if we consider the imperatives of individuation, and the psyche's tendency to help the individual *open up* and actualize him/herself. Once again, we have the concept of a local chaos in a global order. The Other confronts us with our shadow and our potential for change. Deep changes in our personality always involve the shadow. And we get in touch with this shadow in a spectacular way when we fall for impossible love. This is what we mean when we say that these encounters, occurring as they do at synchronistic moments, are 'catalyzing' encounters. By entering into a relationship with our shadow, we are moved to bring lasting changes to our personality. In an exceptional way, some of

---

72 Jan Bauer, *Impossible Love: Or why the heart must go wrong,* Spring Publications, Putnam, CT, 1993.

these encounters can develop into lasting relationships. But as a general rule, to insist on maintaining these sorts of relationships in real life is to continue to perpetuate a distancing effect within oneself. It is only when we are able to grasp the symbolic import of these impossible loves, that they can become opportunities for transformation.

The meaning of metamorphosis

We may wonder if we need to be conscious of synchronicity in order for it to operate and be able to transform us.

There are probably synchronicities that escape our consciousness. One of the consequences of these significant coincidences or synchronistic encounters is precisely to expand consciousness to a greater vision of self and the world. But in order to expand consciousness, we need to perceive meanings beyond what can be accomplished through rational thought. Meanings are especially effective due to their emotional impact. Even though we may not always know the motives of our emotional responses when synchronicity occurs, we can assume that something is at work here, as when we are moved and fascinated by a person we meet casually.

The same thing occurs when we dream. Even though some of the meanings may escape us, dreams prompt us to react by means of the emotional energy they generate. The more we manage to become aware of this meaning, the greater the power of transformation. Moreover, by becoming conscious of the symbol's meaning, we will avoid falling into repetitive symptoms.

The symbolic impulse stemming from synchronicity normally leads to a state of flux, a quest for meaning, even though we may not be fully aware of what is at stake during these very meaningful experiences. The impact of meaning therefore goes beyond rationality and transforms the personality on a number of levels.

The pathology of meaning

Sometimes we look for meaning by relying solely on our reason. The search for meaning can therefore become an obsession when in fact the meaning of synchronicity has an almost exclusively irrational foundation. In addition, the many coincidences in our life are not all synchronistic. If we were to interpret every pot we break as a sign to 'break up' a relationship, the divorce rate would get even worse!

When we perceive meanings in a pathological way, we are relying on our selective attention and our rationality. When a coincidence occurs, we often react like the person with a hammer in his hands who sees nails everywhere he looks. Everything can be potentially significant, of course, that doesn't mean we must find meaning in everything. Synchronicity is an inherent property of life that reflects the perfect symmetry between the outside and the inner worlds; but we cannot possibly live in this state of fusion with the universe at all times. Very often, we mistake our coincidences for our wishes, and we interpret reality according to our own desires. By constantly looking at traffic signs and searching for signs everywhere, we may end up driving off the road.

We can 'corrupt' synchronicity by persistently repeating phrases like: 'Why is this happening to me?' When we look for the meaning of synchronicity, we don't come up with reasons or logical causes; it is rather a meaning, a direction founded mainly on intuition. The question we need to address following a meaningful coincidence is the following: 'Where is this going to lead me?' or, as Jan Bauer writes in *Impossible Love*, 'What will come of this?'

In our relationships, for example, the meaning of synchronicity, when developed on a purely rational level, can be misdirected to manipulate the other person. In the hands of a manipulator, the meaning of a synchronistic event may be analyzed to his/her advantage leading to such interpretations as 'What you are living is not a coincidence' or 'Such an event has a meaning that only I know'. In fact, part of the meaning of synchronicity will always escape us. Very often, the meaning we give to it is deeply challenging; that is why it may be difficult to integrate.

More generally, the weakness of our symbolic life and the stunting of our imagination (when for example we take everything at face value) can lead to great excesses and encourage a symptomatic lifestyle. When we are hungry, we eat too much; when we want more love, we make love compulsively; and when we want more power, we are ready to 'buy' anything. All this will never satisfy the deep desire we have. By transforming our desires into needs, we condemn ourselves to never being satisfied. We want it all, even when we don't need it, because our needs are subjected to the infinite laws of desire. When we take the messages of consumer society 'literally,' we are indeed constantly unsatisfied. The archetype of wholeness, the Self, is perverted by our consumer needs and by this frantic quest to have 'everything'.

American Beauty

The film *American Beauty* touches on several interesting aspects of the pathology of meaning in a consumer society. In this film, we see how material possessions can become an obsession and an illusion by denying us our freedom. In one episode of the radio show *Projections*, the sociologist, lawyer and writer Robert Jasmin used the characters in this film to analyze the loss of meaning that characterizes our Western society. Here, obsessive consumption becomes a frantic quest to fill an expanding and intolerable void. In one of the scenes of the film, probably one of the most moving scenes in American cinema, we see an empty plastic bag blowing in the wind for several minutes. As a symbol of consumption, this plastic bag represents the lightness of things, and the beauty of simplicity.[73]

Caroline, the wife of Lester Boorman, is also overtaken by this obsession for luxury objects. At a crucial point in the film, she listens to an audiotape on assertiveness in the car. She returns from this trip with a plan to kill her husband. The film symbolically demonstrates how simple tips for personal growth are sometimes acquired by consumer society, cutting off and 'killing' creative impulses, as we see with this woman and her husband. This man symbolizes the rebel looking for change. His spontaneous gesture for love is thwarted by his wife. In a scene in which love could have been possible for them, she turns him down for fear of staining her couch.

'Be perfect!'

'It is better to be whole than perfect,' said Jung. When I walk into a bookstore these days, I feel extremely weary as I scan through all the books I am 'supposed' to read to be happy. There are so many books to read, so many things we are suppose to know in order to find happiness. We have never had so many 'guides' to tell us which direction to take. I question the relevance of the motto: 'Find happiness at all costs!' that has subtly made its way into our society and may end up stifling our creativity. Personal growth is all too often just another way of consuming and can easily become pop psychology.

These typical messages increasingly filter through our relationship with ourselves. As Pascal Bruckner so justly points out in his book

---

73 Analysis broadcast during the radio show *Projections* of July 4, 2000 (CKRL-FM).

L'euphorie perpétuelle: Essai sur le devoir de bonheur,[74] happiness has become a necessity and a collective drug: 'Be happy. And be perfect!' Bruckner adds: 'We can of course cure certain illnesses but not unhappiness itself.'[75] Of course, we can take advantage of useful tools for increasing our spiritual growth; but the message conveyed is that of an obsession to live a perfect life, one in which all hardships are eliminated and 'dealt with' in a definitive way. In this atmosphere of perpetual improvement, acquiring self-esteem has become quite a challenge these days. There is always one more workshop claiming it will make us even better. 'Reach perfection in one weekend. No payment necessary until March,' goes the claim. When we consider that our relationship to ourselves and to others is often a source of tension, it may seem easier to stop paying attention and start zapping with the remote control, rather than taking up the challenge to try to improve faulty communications. Maintaining the illusion that one day our lives will be completely rid of suffering is a one-way guilt trip.

Intellectual abuse

This pathology of meaning in the area of personal growth appears in an especially subtle form as intellectual abuse.[76] This consists in giving information or teaching something to someone who is not ready to integrate it. In the case of synchronicity, intellectual abuse consists in imposing an interpretation that the subject is as yet unable to assume. These types of abuse lead the individual to interpret signs literally, by relying only on outside events and ignoring his/her ability to question these events. It can lead to a stunting of the imagination typical of our increasingly media-permeated society, one that dissects information into little pieces before making us swallow them. It is futile to force an interpretation of synchronicity on someone who does not wish to receive or integrate it. A dream without an interpretation is like an unread letter. When this happens, it is like receiving a personal letter that someone else has opened and changed all the words, without us realizing it.

It is not always easy to integrate information that comes from a synchronicity. It involves working on your personality, and very often

---

74 Pascal Bruckner, *L'euphorie perpétuelle: Essai sur le devoir de bonheur*, Grasset, Paris, 2000.

75 Ibid.

76 This idea of intellectual abuse was developed by Jean Bédard during a seminar on Nicholas of Cusa in the summer of 1999 in Bic, Quebec.

---

requires that you give up certitudes and the comfort of a possibly stable and perfectly ordered life.

The transformation brought about by synchronicity is of course not easy to follow as it very often prompts a change, a sort of metamorphosis of our deepest being. But a synchronistic vision of the world allows us to escape the programming and conditioning typical of a consumer society. Synchronicity brings a well of creativity to our lives and frees up space for play. And this play space between real life and the imaginary is where the archetypal figure of the Trickster takes up residence.

Chapter 7

Between Two States

This world is but a bridge. Cross it but
Do not build your house there.
  Henn, Apocryphes, 35

Until tonight, you thought life was absurd.
From now on, you know that it is mysterious.
  Eric-Emmanuel Schmitt, *Le Visiteur*

After several security checks and a long expedition in the Western Sahara, I finally reached Cape Juby, an outpost in the southwest part of Morocco. The hotel attendant told me he had not seen any Canadian tourists here for eight years.

Room 7 in Hotel Tarfaya, where I took up residence for a few days, looked more like a prison cell than a hotel room—the bed, if we could call it that, was full of holes and exposed springs. But this quiet, little village, spread between the massive dunes of the Western Sahara and the choppy waves of the Atlantic Ocean, nevertheless had an exotic charm. A Spanish fort dominates the village and an abandoned prison watches over an island a few hundred meters from the endless beach. I could walk for hours on end without meeting anyone on the beach. From time to time, I came upon a few old, rusty ships, probably beached many years ago. When it was too warm, I went to the beach; when I was cold, I returned to the dunes.

This seemingly uninteresting little village has an important place in history. Cape Juby was a mail stopover point for North Africa, and Antoine de Saint-Exupéry was in charge of this post during the glorious days of the Aéropostale. In those days, mail was taken seriously, due to the long and treacherous routes taken by the airborne pioneers. The Moors often intercepted this mail and used it as blackmail, to recover land the

Spanish had taken from them. Airplane pilots were often tortured and killed.

When I think of Cape Juby, I think of the perils faced by the Aéropostale pilots to reach their destination. This place symbolizes difficult in-between states for me. The in-between state is associated with an important figure from mythology: Hermes, the Trickster, patron of travelers and robbers, the mediator and the messenger between the conscious and the unconscious. Interestingly, Hermes was the first name given to an electronic mail system.

This archetypal figure of Hermes, the Trickster, is the embodiment of the unexpected. Indeed, when we travel, we expect the unexpected in a way, and we are more receptive to synchronicity. No need to go very far, though, to get caught in the net of this archetype of movement—Hermes the Trickster…

Hermes, Mercury or the Trickster

Despite the many theories we come up with to explain synchronicity, we must remain modest and keep an open mind when it comes to the spontaneity of the Trickster archetype and significant coincidences. Synchronicity's very erratic behavior is due partly to this archetype of the Trickster, associated with Hermes.

In mythology, figures embody universal properties. This is one of Jung's most fascinating discoveries: he identified a number of recurring patterns in the traditions of several peoples who had never been in contact with one another. Among these archetypes is the figure of Hermes or for the Romans, Mercury.

According to the alchemists, the substance mercury was a sort of dry water, impossible to grasp and undifferentiated. Hermes is the god of boundaries, the messenger of the gods. He is the one who brings dreams to mortals. He is an underground god, a guider of souls. We associate him with borders, boundaries and transitions. As mentioned previously, Hermes is the god of travelers, robbers and merchants. In Ancient Greece, merchants operated on the borders of villages. Nowadays, we have duty-free shops on the borders of countries. Some border guards seem to be possessed by this archetype of the Trickster when they ask you to empty your luggage before their greedy and curious eyes.

The Trickster is closely related to Hermes and is greedy, egocentric and amoral. He is a troublemaker who upsets established order and wreaks havoc just to have fun. Prairie Indians associate him with the coyote. The coyote is a creator often associated with the creation of culture and the world. In the well-known television show, cartoon characters are used to parody the coyote's cunning as he upsets Road Runner's tranquil existence. He is a Trickster who creates disorder in order to trigger movement.

In Arthurian legends, the Trickster is associated with Merlin, who has a double nature, half man and half devil; conceived by God and the devil, both a luminous and a dark figure; he embodies order and chaos. According to the legend, Merlin appears when you don't need him and disappears when you need him. He steps in, for example, to create discord or reinstate order, always for no apparent reason. But he often intervenes when the situation appears hopeless to us. In the episode where Arthur defiantly breaks Excalibur in his combat with Lancelot, Merlin—in league with the Lady of the Lake—steps in to repair the sword.

The legend also relates that one day Merlin announced that his time was running out, that the spirits of nature like him would make way for the one God and the coming of the reign of Man. Merlin ended his life imprisoned in a crystal slab. This is a beautiful metaphor of an irrational principle that has been officially expelled, making way for the reign of rationality. This principle continues to operate in our daily lives. It represents the element of surprise typical of synchronicity, without logical causes.

African mythology is full of these devious little spirits. For Africans, this archetype is associated with Eshu, the god of timeliness. It is said that he would wait at the entrance and exit of villages, watching the people entering and leaving. Allan Combs, in his book on synchronicity and the Trickster, tells the following amusing story about Eshu.

> Two brothers joined forces to start up a farm. They had decided to share everything, going so far as to dress the same way. Eshu decided he would break this habit: he disguised himself as one of the brothers but dressed differently. When his brother saw him, he was very upset. This incursion by Eshu the Trickster created a dispute between the two brothers. When one of the gods asked him why he had done this, Eshu answered it was only for fun. The story ends with Eshu setting fire to the village, forcing the people to share all their goods once again.[77]

Here, we see how the Trickster goes about making trouble for no apparent reason, then reestablishes a new order. He loves to turn things upside down, only to turn them right side up afterwards.

---

77 Allan Combs and Mark Holland, *Synchronicity: Science, Myth, and the Trickster*, Paragon House, New York, 1990.

The Trickster is also associated with dance and music. In fact, Hermes invented the first lyre using a cow stolen from Apollo's herd. After sacrificing the animal to the gods of Olympus, Hermes returned to his cavern. On the way there, he found an enormous turtle shell. What could he do with this? He had a brilliant idea: he cleaned the entrails of the cow he had just sacrificed and strung them over the hollow part of the shell. He pinched the strings with his fingers and played melodious sounds: the first lyre was born.[78]

The Devil at the Dance and *The Outlander*

When I was small, I was fascinated by stories about devils. At Saint-Jean-Port-Joli, a little village along the Saint Lawrence River, my cousins and uncles would tell stories about the devil. I especially remember the one about the *Flying Canoe*, in which the devil gave a flying canoe to a group of woodsmen so they could return to their wives. They were forbidden to say the word 'God,' however. Of course, this inevitably happened, and the woodsmen would fall to the ground.

The archetype of the Trickster is also present in the Quebec folktale of *The Devil at the Dance*. This Quebecois legend tells the story of the devil who seduced women by dancing with them. He would arrive in the village without notice on a wintry evening, and go into a carefully chosen house. He impressed everyone with his skills and the quickness of his steps—the young ladies were mesmerized. Inevitably, one of these women would fall for his charms and be whisked off. Once again, the typical characteristics of the Trickster are at play: his impromptu visit and the trouble he causes—in this case seducing a woman with his dancing ability.

We also find echoes of this archetype in *The Outlander*,[79] by Germaine Guèvremont, an international best-seller when it was first published in the 1940s. This mysterious character arrives in the village of Chenal du moine one fall evening and upsets the Beauchemin family's daily routine. More recently, the writer Suzanne Jacob, in her book *Rouge mère et fils*, created a similar character that she effectively called 'The Trickster'.

---

78 Odile Gandon, *Dictionnaire de la mythologie grecque et latine*, Hachette, Paris, 1992, p. 235.

79 Germaine Guèvremont, trans. Eric Sutton, *The Outlander*, McGraw-Hill, Toronto, 1950, p. 290.

Jung and the Trickster

Jung was influenced by this archetype while preparing a statistical study on the pairing of couples, based on the positions of Mars and Venus in each partner's star chart. According to Hubert Reeves,[80] this was not the best way to demonstrate synchronicity. Indeed, Jung was somewhat naive in interpreting the statistics. When however he tried repeating the experiment, he realized that the Trickster was playing with his statistical results.

In the fascinating correspondence between Jung and Pauli, we find the concept of 'The Stranger' associated with the spirit of Mercury (Hermes). It appears notably in one letter from Pauli in which he establishes a link between the stranger and radioactivity. According to Pauli, the 'stranger's' goal is to 'transmit a total image of nature.'[81] This is exactly what this archetype sets out to do: force us to expand our perception of the world by playing tricks on us.

The Trickster wants us to *play* and *not take ourselves too seriously*. He embodies both the importance of play and the loss of time. In an increasingly regulated society, the archetype of the Trickster sneaks in and encourages freedom and spontaneity.

When we take ourselves too seriously at the risk of becoming egocentric, the archetype of the Trickster allows us to adjust our vision of the world and fall back to earth. His actions can sometimes appear nonsensical, leading to a break-up in a relationship, or a string of encounters that have no other goal than to get us rolling. This can happen when we start seeing meaning everywhere.

We may have played the role of the Trickster ourselves: by helping someone without realizing it, by chance on a street corner, etc. Very often, we are not aware of the influence we have on people, or the fact that they have been profoundly changed by us. We may have acted as Tricksters for these people. It would certainly be a fascinating task to identify the Tricksters in our life, all these people that have allowed us to 'open ourselves up' spontaneously to a new potential.

Thresholds

Just like synchronicity, the Trickster is closely related to transitional phases of our existence. Major transitions such as adolescence or midlife

---

80 Hubert Reeves, *La synchronicité, l'âme et la science*, op. cit., p. 19.
81 *The Pauli/Jung Letters*, op. cit.

predispose us for synchronistic experiences. Making a career change can sometimes bring about astonishing synchronicities. A person we meet by chance can have a determining impact on our life. We often meet significant people on the 'thresholds' of our life, i.e. in places we don't normally go to, while entering or exiting, departing or arriving, and at turning points in our lives.

The in-between space, the Trickster's playground, is an important dimension for understanding synchronicity. The in-between space is a place where the inside mingles with the outside and vice versa. In a culture where rationality is supreme, it is not surprising that this archetype suddenly makes its appearance; it tends to provide a more global vision of the world by manifesting itself in an acausal and irregular way.

Synchronicity helps us become aware of this intermediate zone that we saw earlier with Winnicott's notion of transitional area. The ancient Egyptians worshipped passages and in-between spaces—the Duat—and even believed they really existed. For them, a Duat was a place crossed by the dead to the beyond, and also where they crossed to reincarnate.

The fear of in-between spaces

When a society has no way of representing this in-between space or state, it may be unable to deal adequately with this type of experience.

This inability to experience in-between states is well symbolized by the psychologist in the film *The Sixth Sense*. This character, played by Bruce Willis, is shot with a handgun at the very beginning of the film, but is unable to realize he is dead. The script is written in such a way that we believe as he does that he is still alive. At certain moments in our lives, we all have this illusion; we believe we are still the same as we were previously. We become like the psychologist in the movie who does not realize that something of great consequence has happened, and tries to avoid change. Something in us dies—we experience a loss for example—and we refuse to admit it by pretending it never happened. We deny the in-between state and, for that reason, are compelled to wander through it indefinitely, just like the character in *The Sixth Sense*.

In-between and anxiety

Anxiety is a need to control and is closely related to this inability to deal with intermediate states. In my profession, I often observe synchronistic events occurring in in-between phases that announce future trans-formations. This is what happened to Lauren.

*Lauren's father was extremely erratic and unpredictable,
and very much responsible for her chronic state of insecurity.
She had a very strict upbringing, with no room for play or
improvisation. Gradually, she began to experience panic
attacks that occurred whenever she went on a trip, especially
when she went by train. In her case, the anxiety was
related to her inability to tolerate in-between states in all
aspects of her life, and particularly in her relationships.*

*One day, she visited a friend who lived more than six hours
away by train. To reduce her anxiety, she got off the train
at each stop to smoke a cigarette. But, while the train was
making a stop (she was at the halfway point), she took longer
than usual to smoke and the ticket inspector refused to let
her back on. At that time of day, she had no choice but to
stay over in this isolated train station. She was forced to
experience an in-between state to the fullest. The meaningful
element she herself brought up in therapy later was the fact
that this city was exactly in-between—she found herself
exactly halfway between her house and her friend's place.*

*This unfortunate incident should have petrified her; instead, she
challenged her attitude concerning in-between situations and
her tendency to avoid them. She explained that this experience
had not worried her at all and that at the time she felt very
calm. What she had found so frightening before, and sought to
avoid at all costs, was embodied in this situation; as a result,
she decided to let go and abandon herself. She considered
this experience to be the signal she needed to examine the
panic situations she was experiencing with an open mind.*

Our inability to tolerate in-between states often expresses itself as a desire to classify and organize everything. The chaotic variations associated with the archetype of the Trickster and synchronicity are precisely opportunities for living with disorder and uncertainty, thanks to the gratuitousness, play and spontaneity conveyed by this archetype. Instability, disorder, and chaos, however, are still part of a dimension of experience that our old Cartesian representations of the world have long neglected.

Chaos and creativity

The Trickster is the personification of chaos. For the Ancient Egyptians, chaos was associated with the deity Set. This civilization brilliantly integrated order and disorder. At the National Museum in Cairo, you can see a magnificent statue of the crowning of Ramses III. The gods of chaos and order, Set and Horus, are standing on either side of the Pharaoh. The god of chaos, Set, is on Ramses' left—the left-hand side has always been associated with disorder and awkwardness (when we say, for example, that someone is *gauche*). But the left-hand side, the side that is seemingly awkward like the Trickster, is a required part of an overall and creative conception of reality.

Chaos is an intermediate phase of flux, a stressful but necessary in-between state that we tend to overlook in our societies. This long, underground voyage is sometimes unpleasant and can seem endless before we reach a new state and a new condition. But in this obscure world of transformations, we find the Trickster, with his recognizable laugh and dancing steps, sends us signals to show us the way out. The Trickster, considered by many traditions to be the archetype of culture, prompts us to move ahead in a creative way. He comes without notice—he comes to take us, as in the legend of *The Devil at the Dance*—and invites us to dance with him. But if we are to accept this invitation and learn to dance, we must not be afraid to give up a little of our tranquility. Each dancing step we take can move us ahead but can also make us fall. The beauty of dance and life resides precisely in this narrow space for play, somewhere between balance and imbalance.

Chapter 8
Places that Haunt Us

We exist in a world with a 'sacred geography,' where a particular spot, house, tree, or view of the sea or mountains becomes a sacred symbol intimately bound up with our love or the loved one.
Francesco Alberoni

Love is not a thing, it is a place.
Réjean Ducharme

In the very first days of March each year, some 200,000 snow geese leave the coast of North Carolina, Maryland and New Jersey to nest in the Canadian High Arctic. But before reaching this destination, located more than 3000 kilometers away, they stop over at Cap Tourmente, near Quebec City. The briny marshes filled with bulrushes attract them there for a well-deserved rest. Then, around the end of May, they start off on the second leg of their voyage. After leaving the riverbanks, they fly over the boreal forest, Hudson Straits, the northern tip of Baffin Island and finally take refuge on Bylot Island to start nesting.

I have always found it fascinating to observe this huge flock of snowy birds recharge their batteries on the banks of the Saint Lawrence in the spring. I am particularly impressed by the memory and spatial orientation capacities of these little creatures. In their lifetime, which lasts about fifteen years, these geese will use the same flight path each year, seek out the same reference points, and battle the same wind currents in the sky to reach this isolated spot in the High Arctic.

Patterns in space

Like these geese, we are mysteriously drawn to certain places. The places that unconsciously attract us very often symbolize our inner state, and transformations in the making. Places to meet, places to live, and places to travel to will be examined in this chapter.

We saw earlier that objects, films, books and music may have a particular significance and become synchronistic motifs in a relationship. This is also the case with places. Places associated with relationships also leave their imprint on the unconscious. If we forget them, the unconscious will see to it that we are reminded of them. It is sometimes very strange to observe a series of coincidences and encounters related to places and city haunts. For example, I ended my first love affair in a coffee shop at the corner of a street in Quebec City. Several years later, I was involved with another woman who lived on the same street. Then, some years after this encounter, I met yet another woman who lived on that same street corner: both women lived only a few yards apart. The unconscious may have been telling me that this place had a significance for me, and that I had not yet accepted my break-up with my first love.

Florence experienced a strange coincidence of this sort in Boston. She had visited the city twice in her life. The first time, she went with a man who wanted to buy a piano in a shop located in an obscure part of the city. This man was particularly important in Florence's life, and the period following their break-up was especially long and painful. Many years later, Florence had practically forgotten this man and was seeing a computer programmer. She went to Boston with her new boyfriend for a computer science convention. Strangely enough, this convention was taking place in a building on the same street corner as the piano store of her former lover! The unconscious had devised this symbolic manifestation—focusing on the piano store—as if to help Florence bring something back to consciousness that perhaps needed to be integrated from her past life.

Symbolic micro-processes of this sort, based on places related to our love affairs, are fairly frequent. A friend of mine told me that after breaking up with a woman who had played a central role in his life, he started seeing another woman several months later. He met her by chance and it turned out she lived right next door to the first woman! These examples illustrate how the unconscious remembers significant places and reminds us of them by bringing up themes and symbols in the key settings of a relationship. Some places are like magnets and are heavily laden with meanings. Places, just like dates, which we will examine in the last chapter, are mysteriously appropriated by our unconscious through meaning and can in that way become 'attractors' for synchronistic events, or become the symbolic stage setting of a future relationship. Exploring the symbolic dimension of places we have a habit of visiting can sometimes help us understand the key issues and motifs of a past or present relationship.

The symbolic settings of our encounters

The physical setting of an encounter sometimes contains the themes and symbols of a future relationship. In a workshop on synchronicity, one female participant mentioned that she met the man of her life in a funeral parlor. She explained that right from the start of their relationship, death had been present in various guises. In the first year of their relationship, both of them had lost several family members. Death had a symbolic value representing a change of state, a passage to another life, and had mysteriously attracted these two persons to meet in this unusual place.

It is fascinating to observe the places where two people have met; in these places, we can sometimes distinguish symbolic manifestations that refer to the necessities of the relationship. It is as if we needed to cross strange, symbolic passageways so as to meet someone.

In relationships, we are very often *chosen* by a place, in the same way that we are *called upon* to find out something about ourselves. It is probably an illusion to believe that we can decide 'where', 'when' and 'how' we will meet that person, as consumer societies would have us believe. A grocery list is as useless as a map for guiding us in relationships. Very often, there is no apparent logic behind these strange attractions that drive us to certain meeting places. We often hear stories like the following: 'I wasn't supposed to be there. In this particular instance, I had to make a detour. I found myself going into this shop and that's where we met...' Or else the following: 'That day, I decided not to take my car to go to work, and while waiting for the bus I met the woman who now shares my life. That morning, she had also decided not to take the car because of the snowstorm expected later in the afternoon.' This illustrates the chaotic aspect of encounters, sometimes resting on a tiny detail, a fraction of a second. Two people find themselves in the same place at the same time: a small fluttering of wings has allowed them to meet and, in many cases, transform their lives forever.

The migrations of the soul

When we let ourselves be intuitively overtaken by meaningful coincidences, we perhaps migrate to the meeting places of our love affairs,
following unconscious signals similar to those followed by geese. Geese
do not question the meaning of their flight, and yet each year they reach
their nesting sites. Moreover, throughout the many years of repeating this
ritual, that is over fifteen years, they always manage to find their original
partner!

It might be a good idea to follow the coincidences and symbolic
markers that lead us to a person. Our intuition is probably the best
compass for guiding us in the 'choice' of a relationship. We think we
move in a rational and individual way—fully in control—but in fact
these movements are probably part of a collective pattern in a vast novel
extending beyond our personal lives. The fluttering wings of migratory
geese, gradually building up one by one into a single group formation in
order to make the crossing, are perhaps like the subtle variations in the
movements of two people that lead them to a meeting place.

Places and memory

For the biologist Rupert Sheldrake, places have a memory, an emotional
and instinctive imprint that can be decoded. Migratory birds may pick
up this information and be able to guide themselves using these intuitive
currents. Certain peoples, such as the Inuit, or nomadic tribes of the
desert, may have nurtured this instinct by recognizing patterns or motifs
that guide them in physical settings. They may be sensitive to the soul of
a place that connects with their own souls.

With this connecting principle through meaning, we call into question the causal relationships that link us to a particular space. But, from
the perspective of synchronicity, a symbolic relation to places indicates
that we are more in interaction with the environment than in control of
that space. To live somewhere is of course to transform the setting, but
in fact that setting acts to transform us even more. Spaces are marked
by history and therefore meaningful. A place is inevitably shaped by the
history that took place there, and this meaning can rise to consciousness
in an episode of synchronicity.

Unfortunately, this symbolic dimension of space was grossly
supplanted during the industrial era, and replaced by a mainly dominat-
ing attitude to space. James Gleick remarks in this context: 'At one time
rain forests, deserts, bush, and badlands represented all that society was

striving to subdue.'[82] John Fowles wrote the following about eighteenth-century England:

> The period had no sympathy with unregulated or primordial nature. It was aggressive wilderness, an ugly and all-invasive reminder of the Fall, of man's eternal exile from the Garden of Eden… Even its natural sciences…remained essentially hostile to wild nature, seeing it only as something to be tamed, classified, utilized, exploited.[83]

Inner experience

If we can access the unconscious of a community by looking at how it arranges its outside environment, we can do the same with individuals. The places we inhabit tell us something about ourselves. We choose a place based on conscious factors, but also unconscious factors that refer to the state of our soul. It is as though certain places mysteriously chose us.

Drawing up a list of all the places where we have lived can become an interesting task. It can sometimes help us connect with the major rites of passage of our life, and the encounters that have punctuated our existence. In his excellent book, entitled *Jung: L'expérience intérieure*, Michel Cazenave conducted an original study of the places where Jung had lived. He found for example that Jung was very much attracted by water from an early age. Already at four, Jung knew he would live close to water one day: 'I thought one could only exist near water.'[84]

For Jung, water and death were closely related. This fact became real to him when, at an early age, he witnessed the drowning of a man in the Rhine. He was fascinated by the blood mixing with the water. What's more, Jung had a vision of the war in the fall of 1913 in the form of a huge pool of blood. This vision coincided with the start of his descent into darkness—the chaos of his unconscious.

It was in a house on the banks of Küssnacht Lake in Zurich, a house built shortly before his meeting with Freud, that he found peace when his unconscious unleashed itself and he began his descent into Nekyia. When his mother died, another place became important for Jung: the

---

82 James Gleick, *Chaos: Making a New Science*, Penguin, New York, 2008, p. 117.

83 Fowles, in Gleick, 2008, p. 117 op. cit.

84 Michel Cazenave, *Jung: L'expérience intérieure*, Éditions du Rocher, Paris, 1997, p. 42.

Bolligen Tower. He built it after freeing himself from this difficult battle with his unconscious. A new residence coincided with a new mental state for Jung.

When his wife died, several years later, he built another tower. The places where Jung lived were thus laden with symbols and marked transitions for him. Strangely enough, his new residence bore the signs of death. During its construction, a body was found near the house located by a lake—that of a French soldier who had drowned there in 1799. This fact is reminiscent of the death of the man in the Rhine. Death, real and imaginary, haunted the places inhabited by Jung.

The construction and furnishing of this tower closely followed Jung's own individuation process at the age of forty-eight. Many incidents occurred during its construction. I will mention one of these in particular—concerning the cornerstone—as it refers to the creative power of chance and synchronicity. Jung wanted to build a dividing wall and ordered a stone to use as a foundation for his house. When the stone arrived, it became apparent that the measurements were incorrect. Jung decided to keep it anyway, associating it with the spirit of Mercury—a creative and unexpected error of sorts. On it he engraved an image of Telesphorus, a figure associated with the Trickster.

Voyages of transformation

Places that attract us can be related to transformations in our life and may be considered synchronistic. We start at point A in order to reach point B, and a transformation occurs between the two. Let's take the example of Jung, who undertook two major voyages. In the first, he visited the Taos Pueblo Indians of New Mexico; in the second one, he went to Africa to see the Elgoni of Kenya, traveling first to Lake Albert and Rejaf in Sudan, up to the city of Khartoum. After these trips—as with his earlier descent into the unconscious—Jung was so transformed that he declared it would take many years for him to assimilate his experiences. He wrote: 'Thus the journey from the heart of Africa to Egypt became, for me, a kind of drama of the birth of light. That drama was intimately connected with me, with my psychology.' This voyage became an inner experience because he was already carrying these places within him—he had made both a real and a symbolic place for them.

The places that fascinate us and prompt us to travel to them can express states of mind or transformations. We can however feel drawn to a place and still visit it as a tourist. Mass tourism is another example of the way modern society perpetuates a vision of space as something that must be possessed and mastered. I'm thinking here of mass tourism as a product of consumer society, which leads to an attitude that is prevalent in several areas. We can act as tourists while on a trip; but we can also behave as tourists when we are with people, or during therapy, by absentmindedly consulting psychologists while barricading ourselves against change.

Lazy tourists constantly carry illusory comfort with them everywhere they go. In fact, they never leave their country of origin and cannot possibly be transformed by a trip or an encounter. 'Unlike the traveler who may never come back, the tourist thinks about his return as soon as he arrives' [my translation, CA], explains Paul Bowles in his book *The Sheltering Sky*.

Encounters while on a trip

Traveling makes us receptive to encounters that may help us unlock a problematic situation. For my part, for a long time, I wanted to come in contact with a discussion group inspired by the work of physicist and philosopher David Bohm. I knew such an association existed in Quebec but I had been unable to find the contact information. At Cairo Airport, just before boarding my plane to Paris, I noticed by the strangest of coincidences a friend from Quebec City, who was a member of this discussion group. He gave me the information I needed while boarding and I learned to my astonishment that this group had an office on the same street as my office in Quebec City!

> *Jean-Sébastien experienced a troubling encounter between flights at Cleveland Airport. Before boarding the plane en route to Montreal, he realized that his seat was located near the mother of his ex-girlfriend—a relationship that he was still trying to recover from. Strangest of all, however, was the fact that he was taking this plane and meeting another woman two years to the day after his girlfriend had left him! This chance occurrence helped him get over a situation that had taken unreal proportions over recent years.*

Airports and train stations are places of transition that foster this type of encounter that seems to obey the laws of necessary chance. This is probably why I like these places so much. I can spend hours in them looking at people meeting or parting. Train stations and airports are places that favor synchronicities, as they are associated with the archetype of the Trickster, the one that tries to get things moving again after a deadlock.

East, west, north, south: Meaning and direction

The cardinal points we take when traveling are symbolic. Traveling east does not have the same meaning as traveling west. The east is where the sun rises. To go east is to return to one's roots, one's origin. When we go east, we follow the archetype for this compass point, i.e. the origin of our story. Somewhere in the unconscious, the repetition of the sunrise in the east and its trajectory towards the west has left its mark.

On the other hand, the west is the place where the sun sets. To go west is to go towards the unknown, the future. The conquest of the west has left its mark also in the unconscious. To go west has always had a connotation of discovery, of pioneering. For the North American explorers of the last century, this conquest meant the search for gold and riches.

Going south means to go to rest. This region is more closely associated with warmth and vacations. According to the author Jean Désy, this direction is connected with civilization, a civilization that has possibly lost its directions.

The north is associated with orientation, direction and transcendence. For example, the French expression *perdre le nord* (to lose the north) is used to signify a loss of orientation in our life—to lose one's wits in a way. We can draw an interesting analogy here with the absence of meaning in our western societies and the gradual loss of direction. It is as if we were collectively 'losing the north' in two senses: on the one hand, in a down-to-earth way through the depletion of the ozone layer and the formation of holes in the layer above the poles; on the other hand, through the loss of meaning that follows from this. The burning sun of technology may not only be diminishing our spiritual direction, but also our global compass point.

Places that summon

Certain places in particular attract us in a way different from the geographic sense. A scene from a film, the writings of an author, a photograph of an unknown country can give off a strong intuitive energy and makes us feel summoned. Something that we perceive in a setting may coincide with an inner impulse; and so we pack up and leave on a whim, annoying our close ones who don't understand why we have suddenly become traveling poets.

True love stories begin in a certain setting. There are voyages that leave their mark forever. Several years may be required before we can fully integrate their meaning—just as it takes time to integrate the meaning of a significant other coming into our life. These voyages prompt us to develop a symbolic relation to space and the world. These symbols take root in the seemingly trivial details of our life settings and can often escape us. It may not always be by chance that we feel attracted to a place and that we find ourselves going to at a certain point in our life. We migrate to these places, as we move towards another person, through the force of meaning, the driving factor behind synchronicity. We go there to establish an encounter with the deeper facets of our identity.

The timing of a trip, like its symbolic properties, can be considered a synchronistic reference to something occurring within us. By listing our voyages and making references to the context, we can discover elements of transformation that have made us grow as a person.

Snowflakes in the desert

We all have our mythical destinations, these places that we idealize and that haunt us. Just as men have within themselves a representation of the ideal woman, the anima, we all have an iconic image of Egypt, the Sphinx, Greece, the Parthenon, etc. But reality never quite corresponds to the representation we have forged. To visit a place with our soul, we must go beyond postcard images and expect to be surprised. What is essential is the process, the voyage much more so than the destination. The voyage will always harbor something that is lacking in the destination—just as the meaning of synchronicity is in a state of flux that we cannot fully pin down. In a voyage, this may simply be a detail, a particular gaze, a child's smile, the image of an isolated place that we will bring back with our luggage… In a voyage, as in synchronicity, it is a matter of looking and taking our bearings.

Mount Sinai and the Egyptian Pyramids were two deeply mythical places for me, the images of two perfect and idealized women. But the reality of the place was very different from my dreams. For example, I climbed the mountain at night amid a string of souvenir shops of all kinds—the only thing missing was a chocolate version of Moses' Tablets of Stone! At the summit, an impressive crowd had gathered. People had come here to see the sunrise and take photographs. Once or twice a year, though, the sky is cloudy, and this was one of those nights. This place, known for its sunrises, had snubbed us. We were all invited to live another experience.

During the descent, it starting snowing and I was not at all prepared for this. This was a profoundly surprising experience for me to climb down Mount Sinai covered in snow, stiff from the cold and completely soaked. It was a strange purification experience.

During my visit to the Pyramids for the event to celebrate the new millennium, a fog hung over the entire area. For many, this unexpected fog was a sad affair that threatened to put a damper on what was meant to be a spectacular visual event. On the other hand it added an unbelievably mysterious aspect to this magical night. After the crowd had left the Giza Plateau during the intermission, at about two in the morning, I had a unique chance to climb Menkaure's Pyramid. Thanks to this unwelcome fog, I was able to spend the first moments of the year 2000 at the summit of this pyramid.

It was a fabulous experience for me to stand on top of this wonder of the world, during a symbolically crucial phase in my life. But in order to live this moment to the full, I had to give up my dream vision of a cloudless night. By giving up my image of perfection about which I had so fantasized, I was able to make myself receptive to the unexpected—this memorable ascension.

At about five in the morning, it started to rain. And, as unbelievable as this may seem, a few snowflakes starting falling shortly before dawn. A climb to the top of a pyramid and a flurry of snowflakes in the desert on New Year's Eve—the eve of a new century, a new millennium—was as unlikely and unbelievable as *Magnolia's* raining frogs. And yet…

Chapter 9
The Other Within Me: Transgenerational Life Themes

I feel very strongly that I am under the influence of things or questions that were left incomplete and unanswered by my parents and grandparents and more distant ancestors. It has always seemed to me that I had to answer questions which fate had posed to my forefathers.
  Carl Gustav Jung

We may be through with the past, but the past ain't through with us.
  Line from the film *Magnolia*

When I reached Aswan, Egypt started looking more like my dreams. To arrive, I had to travel the full length of the Nile, a slow trek through time and history. On the banks of the sacred river, inhabitants went about their daily affairs; they patiently tilled the land, impervious to the passage of time and ignoring the noisy tourists from another century. The ancestors of these peasants from the Nile had witnessed the passage of illustrious people. It was on this fabulous river that Cleopatra fell in love with Caesar, probably on their memorable cruise that led them to the temple of Philae, located on the small island near Aswan. This temple was once dedicated to the queen's favorite goddess: Isis.

The first encounter between Cleopatra and Caesar was particularly symbolic. Due to the political instability of Alexandria, Cleopatra was living in exile in the desert before meeting Caesar. To meet him and avoid being ambushed by her enemies, Cleopatra was forced to hide inside a carpet. The very passionate love affair that ensued changed history. As is often the case, love divides what was once united and unites what was once separated. This relationship led to a major division in the Roman world. After the murder of Caesar, carried out by conspirators who disapproved of this union, Octavius led the famous Battle of Actium against Cleopatra and Mark Antony. The latter's humiliating defeat allowed the great Roman family to extend their territory to the other side of the Mediterranean.

The long, ancient history of the Pharaohs ended with the reign of Cleopatra, last link in the Ptolemaic Dynasty. A long tradition disappeared beneath the marching steps of the new conquerors, who trod on a carpet symbolically rolled out by the Egyptian queen. This queen left an indelible mark in history. To preserve her dignity and that of her ancestors, she ended her life with an asp bite, and returned to the sea of immortality. Cleopatra's body has never been found. Her remains probably rest somewhere in the sea near Alexandria, at the mouth of the Nile. Since that time, her soul guides those who set sail on the sacred river.

Patterns over the course of time

The subtle and repetitive patterns that form over the course of time are somewhat like eddies in a river. What's more, the representation of time as we know it today is closely related to rivers. Spring floods in the Nile, for example, both a blessing and a hazard, are the origins of the first calendar and the first measure of the passing seasons. Once a year, the river swells with water from Ethiopian monsoon rains and spreads a blackish mud over its banks—the Black Land of the Egyptians. This rich silt, probably the most fertile on Earth, relies on the unpredictable forces of the Nile and its mysterious currents. When flooding is excessive, entire villages are destroyed; insufficient flooding leads to famine.

To avoid becoming the plaything of fate, but also to try and mark down the passage of the seasons, the ancient Egyptians created the world's first calendar, based on three four-month seasons. They established this calendar by observing when floodwaters covered the riverbanks, and when the water receded. It is based on this model that calendars are still established today.

Our own existence is also subject to unpredictable flooding. We constantly try to predict these periods to avoid them; nevertheless, subtle and uncontrollable currents from the depths sometimes rise to the surface. They may take the form of themes that repeat themselves over time within the same family. Family myths are related to what Anne Ancelin Shützenberger calls the Ancestor Syndrome, in her book 'Aïe mes aïeux!'.

One participant at a workshop on synchronicity told the story of a cousin who had died after a serious illness one year to the day after her sister, who had committed suicide. Date coincidences within a family are more common than we might think. It is as if the unconscious remembers important milestones in family history and is jogging our memory by creating a signifying order through coincidences.

The anniversary syndrome

The unconscious has an excellent memory. It marks important events using small lifebuoys that it places here and there on our life stream. These markers, warning us of eddies in our personal story, are at the heart of key events, such as repeated accidents or congenital diseases. These repetitions mysteriously occur on the same dates, at the same ages. It is common, for example, to find an individual developing cancer at the same age as another member of the family. Births can also occur on the anniversary of the death of a person from the same family.

Camille, for example, had two children. Jean, her firstborn, was born on June 15, 1965, and died at eleven months from birth complications. Mathilde, her other child, gave birth to a son Benjamin on June 15, 1990, twenty-five years to the day after the birth of Jean. Moreover, Benjamin and Jean were born three minutes apart, after a twenty-five-year interval!

The synchronistic aspect of these coincidences has to do with the meaning that links these events together, in the aftermath of a family drama. In these cases, the unconscious uses attention-grabbing coincidences in dates to reveal an important motif in our story. Our lives are filled with periods and dates that mark us profoundly and these are stored as thematic motifs in the unconscious.

Certain dates and certain periods of the year are often tainted with sadness. For example, one year after ending a love affair or experiencing some other misfortune, we may feel melancholy each time we relive this period of the year. We are influenced by moods of an unknown origin that reveal vulnerable aspects of our personal story, the bad times, the strokes of bad luck.

Simone de Beauvoir died the night of April 15, 1986, the anniversary of the death of Jean-Paul Sartre (April 15, 1980), the man who had meant the most to her in her life. She died a few years after him, on the same date, during the night, with a few hours difference. Meaning seems to defy the rational principle of causality here by linking her death to the man who had been her life companion.

By examining the events that have marked family history, we often find the source of these black periods that recur in our own lives at certain times of the year. John F. Kennedy 'chose' not to use the bulletproof roof of his car in Dallas on November 22, 1963. He was not aware of the death threats against him, but he especially 'forgot' that his great-grandfather Patrick died on November 22 (1858).

Transmitting traumas

It is surprising to realize the ways in which the unconscious can influence the course of events by arranging them into a narrative sequence. Schützenberger even mentions the possibility that certain car accidents can be influenced by family history.[85] She gives the example of a 28-year-old nurse who had a car accident with her four-year-old daughter. Surprisingly, this woman had been in a car accident on the same road at the same place when she herself was four years old.

She also gives the example of a 27-year-old doctor[86] who had a car accident on Mozart Street in Paris, while driving his six-year-old son to his first day of school. Again, he had also been in a car accident when he was six, on this same street during the same period, while going to his first day of school with his father. Back to school time was for him and for his entire family a time of great tensions and extreme vulnerability.

Should we conclude that a vulnerable state can make someone more accident-prone, as if trauma was a contagious disease? Susan Mirow,[87] psychiatrist and professor of psychiatry with the Department of Medicine at the University of Utah, has been studying ultradian rhythms of people who have experienced traumatic events. Ultradian rhythms are rhythms that function within a 24-hour period and are found in all living organisms. They regulate our biological functions somewhat like a clock, synchronizing the rhythms of cell reproduction, heartbeats, breathing, sleep and so on. The regulation and flexibility of these rhythms have a great influence on our psychological state and social relationships.

---

85 Anne Ancelin Schützenberger, *Aïe, mes aïeux! Liens transgénérationnels, secrets de famille, syndrome d'anniversaire et pratique du génosociogramme*, Épi/La Méridienne, Paris p. 128.

86 Ibid, p. 128.

87 Susan Mirow, 'Co-morbidity of Post-traumatic Stress Disorder and Obsessive Compulsive Disorder: Affect and Regulation and Chaos Theory,' paper presented at the 9th annual convention of the Society for Chaos Theory in Psychology and Life Sciences in Berkeley, 1999.

Mirow measured the ultradian rhythms of people who had suffered trauma and found their complexity to be significantly reduced. Over time, these subjects react through an increased rigidity or mechanization of these rhythms. This rigidity is a sign of illness and poor adaptation; just as we saw in Chapter 4 how a heartbeat that is too mechanical can lead to death. What is most interesting about Mirow's discovery is that the rigidity and shape of these ultradian rhythms are transmitted over generations.[88]

One of the characteristics of trauma is repetition: a person who lives through a traumatic event will constantly relive it, either by becoming phobic or by having the same nightmares over and over again. In a holistic and systemic perspective, these nightmarish repetitions could become life themes that people who have suffered trauma transmit to their children.

By measuring these rhythms, we are able to produce a record of how trauma is handed down—a family's *unfinished business*, as it were. Incredibly, this rigidity may become manifest in the details of objective events—when, for example, accidents thematically repeat themselves in times of heightened vulnerability. In these cases, we unconsciously tick according to a kind of family clock and unwillingly reproduce family dramas on precisely the same dates.

By searching through personal and family history, we find themes that repeat misfortunes, and coincidences that are sometimes dramatic. Accidents, illness and death mechanically follow the shape of these attraction points that are based on dates and times of the year; they are without a doubt the most mysterious manifestations of an 'unconscious family loyalty'.

Unconscious family loyalty

Unconscious family loyalty is one of the key concepts developed by Hungarian psychiatrist Ivan Boszormenyi-Nagy, cofounder of the transgenerational approach. According to this concept, a family has 'family accounts' that are handed down from generation to generation. Children must unconsciously account for what they receive from their parents, in keeping with an unconscious family loyalty. This loyalty is founded on

---

88 Susan Mirow, 'Intergenerational Transmission of Trauma: Ultraradian Rhythms as Biological Transducers,' paper presented to the European Society of Traumatic Stress Studies, Turkey, 1998.

the sum of assets that a family possesses. If the family accumulate unpaid bills, the children inherit debts.

I had a client who used the expression 'pay his bills' when referring to these family accounts he kept with his mother. He told me he was under the impression that his mother loved him as long as he 'paid his bills,' i.e. did what his mother requested of him to be loved in return. More often than not, this bill was unconscious. The family debt builds up through strict and rigid behavioral patterns and unconscious repetitions.

One of the manifestations of family loyalty is what Vincent de Gaulejac[89] calls *class neurosis*. Class neurosis is a moral obligation not to exceed the social status of an individual's family in order to maintain family loyalty. The typical case is that of a student from a working-class family who, just before a bar exam, develops a terrible ache in his stomach. In more dramatic cases, individuals fail their exams over and over again, unable to free themselves from this invisible loyalty.

Forced celibacy and symbolic lifelines

A similar phenomenon occurs when we avoid encounters for unconscious reasons. Celibacy, for example, may be based on a repressed motive of unconscious loyalty towards a father or mother who enforces implicit family rules. We can 'beat around' a fixed and uncreative attractor in this way by repeating a pattern imposed by family myth. Some people miss all their appointments. Or else, when a friend sets them up with a potential match, they suddenly develop all kinds of problems. Another example is the young man who is excessively attached to his mother and turns down all dating opportunities, or enters into impossible relationships with women. Sometimes, a woman may wait for her mother to die before welcoming a chance event that 'mysteriously' places a man on her path.

We can observe how the unconscious works through the repetition of these faulty life scenarios. It sometimes takes several repetitions before recognizing the underlying themes to these life scenarios. Date repetitions and coincidences are both repetitions and attempts at healing. In psychology, we speak of the three Rs: Repeat, Recognize, and finally Remedy. Repeating unconscious family scenarios is part of symbolic micro-processes that can become conscious. If we are aware of them, they can be like navigation buoys, indicating dangerous currents and showing the way.

---

89 Vincent de Gaulejac, *L'histoire en heritage: Roman familial et trajectoire sociale*, Desclée de Brouwer, Paris, 1999.

Typical synchronicity, with its potent force of meaning, is more like a lighthouse than a navigation buoy: a lighthouse that towers over our path and tries to radically deflect our life trajectory when the risk of shipwreck becomes too great.

A tool to identify life motifs

The repetition of life themes is an important component of this book. The synchronous chart of our family events[90] can be useful in helping us to identify these repetitions. To draw up this chart, ask your parents and grandparents to tell you the important dates of your family history, as well as those that correspond to specific events. The synchronous chart allows you to identify milestones in the life of a parent, brother, or sister and put these events in parallel with your own life. (When did these events occur? How? Did we experience the same thing at the same age? etc.) It will thus be easier to bring this unconscious loyalty to consciousness and see the repetitive patterns that emerge from your family myth.

For example, a mysterious sequence of events from the past can help us understand how three sisters became pregnant at the same age, at about the same date, and with the same time interval between meeting their partner and becoming pregnant.

We hope never to repeat the errors of our parents. And yet, we sometimes find ourselves acting out the same scenarios, especially when it comes to relationships. Drawing up a chart of our relationships can be enlightening. Who are the important people in my life? At what period in my life did I meet them? What were the symbolic background elements and settings of these encounters? Can I make parallels with the way in which my parents and grandparents met?

Sophie, for example, discovered sometime after meeting Alexandre that both had a great-grandfather 'born of unknown father'. This black hole in their family tree made both of them feel ashamed. It was this carefully hidden family secret that united them. On the other hand, though neither one was sterile, this same secret unconsciously prevented them from conceiving a child … descended from a 'bastard'.

---

90 Proposed by Anne Ancelin Schützenberger, *Aïe mes aïeux!*, op. cit., p. 50.

Les enfantômes[91]

Replacement children are another example of the many mysterious repetitions of unconscious loyalty. Replacement children are those children who are born precisely on the date at which another child from the same family died. The mother's unconscious seems to project itself into the unconscious of the future child. For example, Vincent Van Gogh appears to have been a 'replacement child'. The famous painter was born on March 30, 1853, one year to the day after the death of another Vincent, his older brother, whom the family never talked about. Vincent Van Gogh had to bear this burden (replacing his brother) all by himself, which no doubt contributed to his tragic destiny.

A premature death leaves traces in the unconscious and this traumatic event continues to haunt the family. The term 'ghost' has been used by two Freudian psychoanalysts of Hungarian descent, Nicolas Abraham and Maria Torök, to illustrate this phenomenon. According to these authors, 'the ghost is a creation of the unconscious that has the distinction of never having been conscious.'[92] A ghost is the handing down of a secret from one unconscious to another. The person receiving the secret does not know the secret—often a shameful secret—but will be unconsciously haunted by this ghost. Saint Augustine said on this subject: 'The dead are invisible, not absent.'[93] Taking care of the dead when we ourselves are alive can help bury them once and for all and silence their manipulative voices.

Magnolia

The film *Magnolia* deals with unconscious loyalty. The psychoanalyst Pierre Ringuette[94] gave a brilliant analysis of this film on a radio show, focusing on the conflicts experienced by parents and handed down to their children. At the very beginning of the film, we see a policeman who finds a body hidden in a closet—an explicit image of something shameful that has been hidden somewhere. What's more, at the start of the film, the narrator lists a series of coincidences, including one incident caused

---

91 Title of a novel by Réjean Ducharme. It is a combination of *enfants* (children) and *fantômes* (ghosts), or ghost children.

92 Abraham and Török, *L'écorce et le noyau*, quoted in *Aïe mes aïeux!*, p. 429.

93 Anne Ancelin Schützenberger, *Aïe, mes aïeux !*, op. cit., p. 1.

94 Taken from the radio program *Projections* of August 22, 2000 with Pierre Ringuette on the radio station CKRL-FM in Quebec City.

by a quarrel between husband and wife. This woman accidentally shoots her son just as he is throwing himself from the roof of his apartment building to commit suicide. Incredibly, the bullet hits him and kills him just as he is whirling by the window of the apartment where his parents are quarreling.

Here is a potent symbolic illustration of a conflict between parents that impacts on the life of their son. Indeed, he has decided to commit suicide—a violent means of putting an end to the unresolved family conflict. Note that in the film, the young man loads the gun used for his own murder. He does this in the hopes that his mother will actually end up shooting her husband during one of their endless quarrels. The French writer Gilbert Cesbron wrote this phrase that sums up the film: 'The arrow that killed the bird had been fletched with its father's feathers.'

The entire film *Magnolia* revolves around this idea of unresolved conflicts between parents, conflicts that resurface in the lives of the children. In the quiz game scene, for example, a symbolic battle is played out between the parents and children, the object of which is to extract secrets from the children.[95] The quiz host drills the little genius, who is struggling with his father's unrecognized desire to succeed. The child becomes a performing monkey, mechanically pressing buttons on a quiz game. We witness the fully fledged drama of the gifted child, as developed by psychoanalyst Alice Miller.

But the character of the little genius will break away from this abusive relationship with his father by opposing it. During the game, he wets his pants, wreaking havoc and destabilizing all the characters. He rejects this unhealthy relationship and asserts himself as a creative being, rather than the repository of his father's unrecognized desires.

The child's action will be immediately echoed symbolically in the film. Just as each character appears to be at a stalemate, it starts raining frogs—a synchronistic illustration of a transformation that each character will subsequently undergo. Mysteriously, the raining frogs will revitalize the characters' lives, as if each one of these hurt beings had at last found the missing piece in the puzzle. In addition, during this unusual rain, one of the frogs falls on the gun of a character attempting suicide. The frogs put a stop to the repetition of the suicide motif and make a creative contribution by saving the life of this man.

---

95 The title of the quiz game is *What Do Kids Know?*

Rewriting your life theme

We cannot escape the theme of our own story. Luckily, it sometimes rains frogs in our own life, allowing us to re-examine it creatively. The quest for our story through our family history (including of course synchronicity and symbolic micro-processes) makes it easier to develop this creative relationship to the world. 'Man is the product of a history for which he seeks to become the subject,' writes Gaulejac, in his book *L'histoire en heritage*. Only consciousness can make him a subject. Otherwise, he remains a mechanical toy, overtaken by the ebbs and flows of unconscious currents and the repetitive, mechanical laws of fixed attractors. We are not predetermined, linear systems, as described by the classical determinist model based on stiff pendulum movements. Though our personal story derives in part from that of other people, our own creative story enriches that of society.[96]

In a society with its eyes turned to the future and yet disturbed about aspects of technological progress, the lack of creative means to deal with the repetitions of history experienced by previous generations has significant consequences. This shriveling up of meaning and the symbolic world, often results in a repetitive and mechanical outburst of violence. What's worse, some of our children are boxed into the programmed roles of robotized consumers, just like the little genius in the film *Magnolia* before the frogs come down as rain.

Seeking out these coincidences in real life and extracting their meaning is of course not an easy task; like a computer we have been taught to interpret everything mechanically at face value. The dwindling of the symbolic world will only become worse in a world where everything is served to us in pre-hashed ready-to-eat format. We must educate our senses and develop ways of perceiving meanings through critical and intuitive observations of meaningful coincidences in our lives and family history. No book, no computer can tell you the significance of coincidences and encounters in your own life. To find these meanings is your job, and part of a unique process of self-actualization.

Our personal symphony starts with themes that are part of a larger story, like a musician who finds himself in the middle of a symphony that is already underway. An encounter between two people is an important part of this story. Two stories are transcended by a larger story; two instruments play in harmony and take part in a work that surpasses them. But it takes time to listen to the motifs of our past history over and over, and

---

96 Vincent de Gaulejac, *L'histoire en heritage: Roman familial et trajectoire sociale*, op. cit., p. 84.

find the right key and the uniquely appropriate way of playing them. If we play off-key, or worse if we mechanically repeat somebody else's notes, the whole symphony will be affected.

We can remain deaf to these symbolic motifs that subtly play themselves out in our relationships. We can ignore the dead bees that land in a loved one's hair after a break-up. We can remain blind to these amazing coincidences that bring us soothing works of art at times when we most need them. We can ignore the clues that guide us towards settings that will be determining for our encounters. We can believe that these meaningful coincidences are just the fruit of an imaginary projection, a weakness in reasoning. We can be convinced that these chance occurrences are not necessary and only happen in books and movies. But by turning our backs on this aspect of reality, we are turning our backs on one of the essential aspects of life: beauty.

Conclusion

Synchronicity is probably the notion that gave rise to the most criticisms of Jung. Most of these critics called him a mystic, and one behaviorist even said that one had to be a little mad to consider such a hypothesis. Of course, synchronicity is not an easy subject to study. As far as I'm concerned, I simply want to advance a few hypotheses on the subject, to the best of my knowledge. This book is above all an exploration into the areas of acausality and the irrational, aimed at showing how a synchronistic and symbolic vision of reality is useful for countervailing the dominant vision of a cold, rational and mechanical world.

Is synchronicity a scientific concept? Given the current state of scientific knowledge, it is difficult to answer in the affirmative. However, science as we know it has only been around for a few hundred years. Like any other myth, science is above all a system of thought capable of explaining the world, based on its own rites and beliefs that vary over time. Science is very useful for answering the major questions of the day. Our era, however, is going through a series of great upheavals, particularly concerning the quest for meaning—an area that still eludes the scientific method.

With its impressive array of specialists and determinists, the god Causality who reigns supreme in the scientific world is starting to be affected by this crisis. With the new science of complexity, chaos theory and breakthroughs in quantum mechanics, we are expanding the parameters of science. It may be that synchronicity will abandon its heretical status and find its way into a new scientific paradigm.

Acausality, or the linking of events through meaning—so dear to the oriental traditions of the Tao—is being increasingly recognized as a necessary means of relating events to encompass the totality of phenomena. Synchronicity is however a principle of gratuitousness that goes against a reason that has been conditioned to calculate and measure everything. This is perhaps why, in a world that is increasingly programmed and has less and less time for spontaneous movements of the soul, it tends to go unnoticed.

This book has maybe come into your life thanks to a friend, after an impromptu visit to the bookstore, or thanks to some other 'chance' event. It has done this at a precise moment, possibly reflecting your current concerns. I hope it will help you start a dialogue with the unknown, the unknown that permeates our life, moves us and questions us—as in *Le Visiteur*.

In a world that tries to reach out to people through networks of all kinds, our daily lives are influenced in their minutest details by a host of unknowns. If I know that my routine existence may depend on a small butterfly effect in a computer in Peking, I may be more apprehensive about my relationships and my illusions of power. The knowledge that significant encounters in life sometimes rest on details that escape the control of reason—meaning that certain persons can completely change my life—can be just as destabilizing.

But to accept chaos, to accept being destabilized, is maybe the way to discover new horizons. Psyche's small, elusive butterfly—the breath that the Greeks so aptly associated with the soul—may be carrying a wind of change that will impact on the furthest and most mysterious reaches of this fascinating world of encounters.